ALL IN TH

TOGETHER

The Unofficial Story of High School Musical

Published by ECW PRESS
2120 Queen Street East, Suite 200, Toronto, Ontario, Canada M4E 1E2

LIBRARY AND ARCHIVES CANADA CATALOGUING IN PUBLICATION

All in this together : the unofficial story of High School Musical.

ISBN 10: 1-55022-764-5
ISBN 13: 978-1-55022-764-2

1. High School Musical (Television Program). I. Title.

PN1992.77.G76A44 2007   791.45′72   C2006-906636-1

Editor: Jennifer Hale
Cover, Text Design, and production: Tania Craan
Cover Image: F. Scott Schafer / Corbis Outline
Printing: Transcontinental

Courtesy Stagedoor Manor: 115–128; Sue Schneider/Moonglow Photos: 13, 18, 21, 25, 32, 36, 38, 40, 59, 63, 80, 86, 107, 133, 134, 140, 141; Albert L. Ortega: 22, 33, 42, 43, 56, 61, 65, 66, 69, 70 (bottom), 73, 87, 97, 98, 102, 104, 105, 106, 110, 137, 138; ML/ Agency Photos: 7, 45, 49, 52, 53, 55, 68, 136; Sthanlee Mirador/ Shooting Star: 8, 9, 20, 31, 39, 57, 62, 89, 113; Rena Durham/ Retna Ltd.: 28, 29, 34, 93, 96; Fred Hayes/ © Disney Channel/ Courtesy: Everett Collection/CP Photo: 17, 71, 100, 101, 143; Howard Wise/Shooting Star: 19, 23, 47, 51, 95; Steven DeFalco/ Shooting Star: 83, 84, 139; Denis Poroy/ CP Photo: 131, 132; Jemal Countess/ WireImage: 11, 70 (top); Christina Radish: 44, 85; Jon McKee/ Retna Ltd.: 74, 111; Phil McCarten/ Reuters/Corbis: 77, 79; INFGoff.com/CP Photo: 15; Eric Neitzel/ WireImage: 16; Effie Naddel/ Shooting Star: 30; Ning Chiu/ZUMA/Corbis: 37; PseudoImage/ Shooting Star: 46; Rune Hallestad/ Corbis: 72; Ron Wolfson/ WireImage: 78; Derek Reed/ Retna Ltd.: 81; Michael Bezjian/ WireImage: 91; Eddie Malluk/ WireImage: 103; Lucas Jackson/ Reuters/ Corbis: 109; Kevin Kane/ WireImage: 112; Chris Walter/ WireImage: 135

This book is set in Minion and Imago

The publication of *All In This Together* has been generously supported by the Canada Council, the Ontario Arts Council, and the Government of Canada through the Book Publishing Industry Development Program.

DISTRIBUTION
CANADA: Jaguar Book Group, 100 Armstrong Ave., Georgetown, ON L7G 5S4
UNITED STATES: Independent Publishers Group, 814 North Franklin St., Chicago, IL 60610

PRINTED AND BOUND IN CANADA

Less than a year ago from the time these words are being written, the names Zac Efron, Vanessa Anne Hudgens, Ashley Tisdale, Corbin Bleu, Monique Coleman and Lucas Grabeel were known to only a select audience. Flash forward to today, and each of them has been elevated to the level of superstar and launched on careers that include feature films and recording contracts. And it's all because of a high school musical.

Correction, not *a* high school musical, but, rather, the Disney Channel original TV movie *High School Musical*, which debuted in January 2006 and created a fervor in its kid, tween and teen audiences. The film broke ratings records and quickly began conquering other media, with songs from its soundtrack resulting in millions of digital downloads from iTunes, the soundtrack disc itself topping the *Billboard* charts *twice*, the eventual DVD moving 1.2 million copies in its first six days of release, an announcement of a sequel for 2007 and the launch of amateur and professional stage versions based on the film.

High School Musical is obviously here to stay.

The real question millions are asking, though, is, "Why?" Why *did* the film strike such a chord with audiences not only in America but around the world as well? No doubt it's a combination of elements, ranging from its appealing cast, the songs that have "instant hit" written all over them (particularly the coda, "We're All in This Together"), director/choreographer Kenny Ortega's innovative dance sequences, and the film's story of young romance told against a backdrop of not giving in to peer pressure and being true to yourself.

Truthfully, any answer offered to that question is nothing more than guesswork. *Nobody* really knows why an audience connects with a piece of entertainment, though it probably is safe to say that *High School Musical* filled a void that its audience wasn't even aware existed, and in doing so has provided a generation with an excuse to sing, dance and rejoice.

What could be a better gift?

THE START OF SOMETHING NEW

"We're writing the book for the first time. We've never had a TV product that's become this big a property so quickly."
— Rich Ross, Disney Channel Worldwide President

When the Disney Channel gave the green light to *High School Musical*, the decision was made to treat this particular TV movie a little bit differently from ones that had preceded it in terms of schedule and budget. More time would be spent making sure that the music was just right, and an increased budget from the Disney Channel norm would ensure that the filmmakers could accomplish what they needed to in order to make it appeal to its intended audience. And given all that has happened since the film premiered a year ago, it really was a decision that has paid incredible dividends.

High School Musical began with executive producer Bill Borden, who had actually produced several films for the Disney Channel, among them *Tiger Cruise* and *A Ring of*

"I used to love watching *Grease* and other movie musicals, and it occurred to me there hadn't been a really good one in a long time."

5

Endless Light, as well as the feature films *La Bamba* and *Play'd: A Hip-Hop Story*.

"I used to love watching *Grease* and other movie musicals," he explains, "and it occurred to me there hadn't been a really good one in a long time. I wondered if we could do the new *West Side Story* or the new *Hair*. One of my favorite movies is *Romeo and Juliet*. And I have three kids. As a family, if you're going to put on movies together and watch them, the ones that keep coming up over and over again are things like *Romeo and Juliet*, *The Sound of Music* and — at least in our house — *Grease*.

"The original concept," he continues, "was to sell this as a feature film. [Executive producer] Barry Rosenbush and I went around trying to sell this as a feature and no one would make it. They kept saying, 'Well, what's the music? Who are the stars?' Then one day Gary Marsh, who's the president of the Disney Channel, and I had a meeting and I said, 'You know, for years I've been wanting to make a *Romeo and Juliet* musical; kind of *Grease*-like with dance.' After a few minutes he said, 'Sounds perfect for us. Let's do it.' If you're going to copy, you might as well copy from the best. We used Shakespeare to inspire us to make this."

Ashley Tisdale with Miley Cyrus, star of *Hannah Montana*.

For the Disney Channel, something like *High School Musical* was a natural progression. The cable network had its beginnings back in 1983, when it was launched as a commercial-free premium channel. In those days, it was a showcase for basic family

Raven, star of *That's So Raven*

Cole and Dylan Sprouse, stars of *The Suite Life of Zack & Cody*

programming representing shows largely from the Disney TV and feature film library. Things had kicked off on April 18 at 7 a.m. with a series called *Good Morning, Mickey*, which consisted of older Disney cartoons featuring its original staple of stars, among them Mickey Mouse, Donald Duck, Goofy and Pluto. Other such compilation shows were accompanied by *Dumbo's Circus* and *Welcome to Pooh Corner*, which (kind of creepily, in retrospect) had humans dressed as characters from the big top and the Hundred Acre Wood who dished out healthy doses of basic morality tales.

Flash forward to 1998, and the Disney Channel went through a bit of evolution in a bid to grow its core audience and to try and take on such networks as Nickelodeon. To accomplish this, its broadcast day was broken into three portions. Preschoolers checked out the morning programming making up "Playhouse Disney." And, then, running from the afternoon to late evening was "Zoog Disney," which was designed for pre-teens and featured original series like *Even Stevens, Lizzie McGuire* (which, of course, pretty much introduced Hilary Duff to the world), *Smart Guy, So Weird* and *The Famous Jett Jackson,* among others. Zoog was also the first attempt by the channel to create a genuine Internet presence for itself by creating a means through which fans could play interactive games and actually see their names broadcast on the channel. For older Disney fans suffering from insomnia, there was the late night "Vault Disney," featuring such classic shows as Zorro and the '50s version of *The Mickey Mouse Club.*

The next evolution came between 2000 and 2002 when Disney's focus really locked on to its different original series, making them the hallmark of the channel, particularly the aforementioned *Lizzie McGuire,* which was becoming a blockbuster hit. More recently, the Disney Channel has continued its winning streak with animated shows *Phil of the Future* and *Kim Possible,* and the sitcoms *That's So Raven* (starring Raven), *The Suite Life of Zack & Cody* (featuring Dylan and Cole Sprouse, Brenda Song and *High School Musical*'s Ashley Tisdale) and *Hannah Montana* (starring Miley Cyrus).

By 2005, with the production of various original movies under Disney Channel's belt (among them Raven's *The Cheetah Girls*), the environment was right for the production of *High School Musical*. What no one could have predicted, of course, was the impact the film would have not only on the Disney Channel itself, but pop culture in general.

NOT STICKING TO THE STATUS QUO

Bill Borden's original concept for *High School Musical* was to take *Romeo and Juliet*, or more precisely a story inspired by it, and place it in a high school. Whereas Shakespeare's original focused on feuding families, this take would concern itself with rival social cliques that do their best to keep a couple apart, not allowing them to pursue their dreams and shake up the status quo.

To transform this concept into a script, Borden and Rosenbush turned to former music journalist turned screenwriter Peter Barsocchini *(Drop Zone, Shadow-Ops)*. Barsocchini, who has a 12-year-old daughter, welcomed the opportunity to work on a project that would appeal to someone her age.

"When they told me Disney was interested in doing a rock musical, I was very excited," he enthuses with a laugh. "It's not hard for me to plug into that high school mentality. High school is such a polarized time. You've got the jocks, the brainiacs, the goths, the drama geeks — everyone has preconceptions about each other. The result in the story is that when the star of the basketball team admits he wants to sing on stage, it turns the school upside down. It's a comedy, but there's a message: don't judge a book by its cover, don't typecast people on campus that you don't know.

"The challenge, in the beginning," Barsocchini continues, "was to find something to write about. You have to find something that's true from your life. I was a jock in high school. And there's a buddy of mine, star athlete, who went on to become a superstar athlete in the NFL and now he's running for governor of Pennsylvania. But in high school, we played basketball together. He had a secret. He had scholarships and everything and came from a tough neighborhood and wouldn't tell anybody his secret. But the truth was, he wanted to be a ballet dancer. And this is Lynn Swann, but he was afraid to tell anyone. So when I was starting to work on the script, I asked the question, 'What if Lynn Swann actually got the courage to admit his secret?'"

He reflects on the fact that a casting director, who had worked on 50 feature films, told him the secret to getting to know an actor beyond the airs they project is to ask them what their high school years were like, to which answers like "I didn't get a date to the prom" are frequent.

"What you come to understand," Barsocchini points out, "is that so much of your life is impacted by that time. Sometimes as adults you discount how big a deal it is for a kid to audition for a high school show or a middle school show. What it means to them. My daughter, who I wrote this for, connected to that idea. Those are big moments for them."

With a way "in" to the story, the producers and screenwriter pitched what they'd come up with to Michael Healy, Senior V.P. of Original Movies at the Disney Channel. He genuinely loved what they had developed and held some sessions with them to flesh out the storyline.

"The theme of teenagers searching for their identity is one that runs, in various forms, throughout Disney Channel's more than 60 original movies," says Healy. "The questions of 'Who am I?' and 'Where do I belong?' are key for kids in the 8 to 14 age

12

group. Our movies are not really about romance; not about violence. They're about identity. If you look at all of them, they're about: 'Who am I? Can I be a kid a little bit longer? Do I have to grow up now? Am I acting too old for my age? Am I acting too young? Can I still be myself and still be with my friends? Do I care what my friends think about me?' All these questions that are sort of pertinent to the kids in the middle-school age group that we go after specifically to try and entertain. And older kids seem to find these questions very pertinent too. I do in my everyday life. So I think what's genius of this is that it doesn't have sword fights. It doesn't have passionate romance. It has a tentative, touching, little first love and a question, 'Can I be with this girl and still be myself?'"

The plot of the film goes something like this: after basketball whiz Troy Bolton and so-called brainiac Gabriella Montez inadvertently meet at a party and end up singing in a karaoke contest together, they feel an instant connection before going their own separate ways. But then they discover that transfer student Gabriella and Troy attend the same school, and the duo decide to audition for the school musical, much to the outrage of drama queen Sharpay Evans and her brother Ryan. All of their friends conspire to keep them apart in an effort to maintain the status quo.

Notes Rosenbush, "You see, there's a certain truth when you see the two characters, Troy and Gabriella. Kids connect to him wanting to get up and do that for her.

So there is a little Shakespeare in that, without all the dying."

What thrilled Barsocchini about the development process was the studio's dedication to the story as the engine that would drive *High School Musical*. "The story came first," he states, "and then the music was created to fit the story. Often in musicals, they'll say, 'We want a song here,' and then come up with a story to fit the song. But Disney wanted the film to focus on the real concerns of high school students in 2005 — which are really not that different from high school students in 1955. Even though it's a comedy, Disney did not want to condescend to kids."

Speaking of comedy, the writer sought advice from Hollywood veteran Garry Marshall, whose long line of credits include everything from the TV series *Happy Days*, *The Odd Couple* and *Mork & Mindy* to such feature films as *The Princess Diaries* and *Runaway Bride*. Reflects Barsocchini, "He told me the key to comedy is to play it for life and death; play it for real. If you go for the joke, it will be corny and no one will care about it. If you go for real, it will be funny or it won't, but people will care."

"It's a comedy, but there's a message: don't judge a book by its cover, don't typecast people on campus that you don't know."

CALLING THE SHOTS
HSM's Director

The development of the script took about nine months and the search went out for a director; a search that didn't have to go farther than acclaimed choreographer/director Kenny Ortega, who had won two Emmy Awards for both directing and choreographing the Opening and Closing Ceremonies of the 2002 Winter Olympics in Salt Lake City, Utah.

He also served as choreographer of the feature films *Dirty Dancing* and *Ferris Bueller's Day Off*, and as director of the films *Newsies* and *Hocus Pocus* and episodes of TV's *Ally McBeal* and *Gilmore Girls*.

"Dance was something I connected with early on," Ortega related to the *Sunday Telegraph Magazine*. "My first recollection of loving it was when I was around three or four years old. I watched my mother and father dancing around the living room. They were swing dancing, because they were war kids. Seeing their happiness in each other's arms, watching my mother twirl and hearing her laughter — it really affected me. Musicals are my greatest love, without question."

Director Kenny Ortega gets a smooch from Vanessa Anne Hudgens and Ashley Tisdale.

In regards to *High School Musical*, he was taken with the idea right from the start. "Young people don't get too many musicals," he explained. "It speaks of the time that they live in. That's what I thought was really fun about this, that we could go back and borrow from the classics, not reinventing the wheel, but do something for young people today who don't have the privilege of having music-driven stories. . . . And I really like the idea of young people coming to know their own voice, regardless of outside pressure from peers, teachers, parents and society. There's too much bullying that goes on and as a result, kids back off from new ideas they have about themselves."

"And I really like the idea of young people coming to know their own voice, regardless of outside pressure from peers, teachers, parents and society."

BOP TO THE TOP
The Music of *HSM*

Let's face it: you can't have a musical without music, and everyone involved knew that without just the right touch in that department, *High School Musical* would have been a flop.

"We had wanted to do a musical for a long time, but we didn't want to do an old-fashioned Broadway musical," Healy explains. "We wanted to reinvent the genre for kids today in a way that would be relevant to their lives, keeping it completely contemporary and identifiable."

Clarifies Barsocchini, "We didn't want to do a musical where someone's eating a sandwich and then bursts into song about the story of their life. What Kenny did was to take the natural circumstances of high school and inject music. For instance, when the basketball team is practicing, there's a hip-hop number. It feels natural, not imposed upon it. For a young audience to relate to it, the music has to fit the moment. Otherwise you're taken out of the story."

A fairly unique approach taken by the producers in terms of the music was not to handle it like a feature film might, with one songwriting team writing all of the songs, but instead they approached a number of individual composers or teams to mix things up a bit. The results were nothing short of amazing. In the end, Matthew Gerrard and Robbie Nevil provided "Start of Something New" (sung by the characters Troy and Gabriella), "I Can't Take My Eyes Off of You" (performed by Troy, Gabriella, Sharpay and Ryan) and perhaps

the film's most popular tune, "We're All in This Together" (sung by the entire cast); David Lawrence and Faye Greenberg wrote "Stick to the Status Quo" (sung by the whole cast); Ray Cham, Greg Cham and Andrew Seeley provided "Get'cha Head in the Game" (sung by Troy); Randy Petersen and Kevin Quinn were represented by "Bop to the Top" (performed by Sharpay and Ryan); Andy Dodd and Adam Watts by "What I've Been Looking For" (also from Sharpay and Ryan); and Jamie Houston by "Breaking Free" (Troy and Gabriella) and "When There Was Me & You" (Gabriella).

Emphasizes Healy, "The songs were all created for the movie and they're written by various songwriters who we know and love. They have done a lot of the music for *Cheetah Girls 2*. They just did a wonderful job. And the songs — I think they speak for themselves in terms of the message. They're just fun songs and we thought they would work, mainly because I remember when we were getting dailies in — where you see what was shot the day before — and we played these in the office. Most of the time, people run the other way when you get to dailies. They're all chopped up and not very interesting to watch. But with these dailies, people would gather around and sing the songs in the corridors. The dailies would disappear. People would show them to their families. We knew we had something kind of special even then."

Admits Ortega, "We put a lot of pressure on the composers. It was important to me that the words were organic to the characters and that they advanced the plot and gave you greater insight into the characters. I'm really pleased they all accomplished that. The music really helps tell the story."

WHO THEY'VE BEEN LOOKING FOR
The Casting Process

With the score underway, the audition process began for the film, with everyone involved searching for just the right actors to play the film's characters. Early on in the production's history, there was some concern of whether it would be possible to find actors who would be able to handle the different requirements that would be demanded of them. For his part, Ortega was pleased to see that this was not as big an issue as everyone had feared.

"A lot of people say the reason they don't make movie musicals is because the talent isn't there in terms of people who can sing, dance and act. That could not be further from the truth. There is a significant level of talent out there, which is maybe even more accomplished than in the past. Dance has evolved in terms of technique over the years, just as acting and athletics have."

One thing the director felt grateful for was the fact that he had the full support of Disney when he made it clear that they could find so-called

19

triple threats for the film, performers who could act, sing and dance (and in some cases a fourth "threat" needed to be added — the ability to play basketball). "For instance," he offers, "for Gabriella, we needed a beautiful, talented actress, but also someone who could really sing. For Sharpay, we needed someone who had great comic skills, but also could belt out a song."

Proving that just about everything regarding *High School Musical* has been different from the norm, Borden points out that when it came time for auditions, they approached things more from the point of view of a Broadway musical than a standard TV movie.

"We brought people in and had them do a scene and read," he says. "Then we selected 25 or 30 who spent eight hours rehearsing in various combinations. It was really like a chorus line audition. In the end, we discovered six fresh faces. A movie like this allows kids that are talented to blossom."

"The audition process starting out was pretty much like any other audition," explains Lucas Grabeel, who came from a theatrical and TV-movie background and who was ultimately chosen to play Ryan Evans, "though it was a lot like a theatrical audition. It was kind of strange to have that kind of set-up in L.A., because I had not auditioned for theater in L.A. yet at that point. So it was a weird throwback, if you will. I got right into it and had a lot of fun, though. It was ambiguous at the beginning regarding what *HSM* was going to be, because we had a short script and did not hear any of the music — there were a lot of holes in the script. One strange thing is the fact that we were singing in the first couple of auditions, just *a cappella* of a song of our choice. When it came down to the top 25 kids for these roles, they had us all come to a dance studio. They spent the entire day

"I distinctly remember Lucas because of what he did the first time out. He did this little song-and-dance number and had so much personality. I was immediately attracted to him to play this role in our movie."

mixing and matching performers. We learned a dance; we all had to prepare a specific song. It was kind of like a Broadway audition. We all sang in front of everybody and danced. The guys that were going out for Troy did a basketball routine and stuff like that. I thought it was just another audition and just went in there and did my thing. A month later, I found out I was cast. It was just a happenstance sort of thing."

Adds Bill Borden, "I distinctly remember Lucas because of what he did the first time out. He did this little song-and-dance number and had so much personality. I was immediately attracted to him to play this role in our movie."

Zac Efron, who had come off the WB series *Summerland* and who would, in the end, be cast in the role of Troy Bolton, notes, "My personal audition experience was exactly like Lucas'. It was like a Broadway-style callback with all of the stages. It was very unique and fun, and I had it easier than some guys at the audition — some of them were passing out! It was seven and a half hours of dancing, singing and acting. And then we had to play basketball. I was probably weakest at that, but I passed. The way it worked is they would watch people audition and tap them on the shoulder and send them home, saying they were no longer needed. I didn't find out I got the part for a week and a half."

Eventually cast in the role of Gabriella Montez, actress Vanessa Anne Hudgens (whose film credits include the critically acclaimed *Thirteen* and the sci-fi adventure *Thunderbirds*) remembers, "In the first audition I went in and did an *a cappella* song. For the second audition, I kind of spaced out and forgot I was going for a musical. When it came time to do the scene, I was, like, 'Oh my God, what am I doing?' So I did the same little piece in the audition and they were, like, 'That was great. Can you sing something else for us?' I sang another part of another song and they were, like, 'That was good, too. Can you sing another thing for us?' Then I sang 'Reflections' from *Mulan* and that was the winner. It was my big concert performance, I guess."

What was interesting to Zac was that while most of the actors auditioning for roles were constantly being switched with different performers to see who had the best chemistry, he and Vanessa found themselves "paired up from the beginning. It was just a random pairing to go through all the stages together, so we were

"That morning,
I was like, I don't care if I'm
the worst dancer or not the best
singer, I'm going to act like the
best dancer and best singer.
I think that's what
I found in Sharpay."

singing . . ." Vanessa quickly adds, "And dancing together for the whole eight hours."

"We hit it off from the beginning," Zac reveals. "We got paired together early in the auditioning process. The casting directors knew somehow. Immediately. We just started having fun. It was an audition. We knew we had a slim shot of getting in, so we just went in and gave it all we could. At the end of the day, our headshots were still together and we were still performing, so everyone else went home and we were still a group. They picked us from the beginning and that was really fun."

Monique Coleman, who had been carving out an impressive resumé with guest appearances on a wide variety of television series, and who was eventually cast as Taylor McKessie, believes that her experience was a bit different from the others.

"It was different because I'm the only character who doesn't sing in the movie," she says. "I originally auditioned for the role of Gabriella and I do have a bit of stage fright that I overcame by doing this movie. I was horrified about it. And at that first *a cappella* audition, I ended up in the corner with my back to the casting director, singing to myself in the corner, because I was so afraid. Then when I was done, I had this feeling that I wouldn't reduce myself to this, so I turned around and said, 'I'm such a better actress than this.'"

She explained that she was actually afraid to sing, but that with time it was something she could get over. Unfortunately for her, she wasn't cast in the role of Gabriella, but, surprisingly, about a month later she was contacted and asked to audition for the role of Taylor, "this snotty little girl who doesn't sing in the whole thing. Thankfully I do have a musical theater background and could already dance and had been dancing since I was really small, so it was a really easy adjustment."

The one person people assume would have the easiest time auditioning for *High School Musical* actually found it the most difficult. Ashley Tisdale, who began her career at the age of three in TV commercials, had appeared on the national tour of Broadway's *Les Miserables* and the international tour of *Annie*, and who was already part of the Disney family portraying Maddie on the hit Disney Channel series *The Suite Life of Zack & Cody*, discovered that initially the powers that be weren't interested in her for the role of Sharpay.

"I actually came in at the very last minute," Ashley recalls. "Casting had said I really wasn't right for the part. I was, like, begging, 'Please, please. I really like the role. I want to come in.' I came in the day before they knew who they were testing. A lot of the kids had the song they had to have prepared for the next day. I kind of came in the day before and met with Kenny Ortega. He really liked me and said, 'I want you to come to the screen test.' I had this huge song to learn and it was really nerve-wracking and I was really uncoordinated with the dance. The amazing thing is that Kenny kind of made us all into dancers. But that morning, I was like, I don't care if I'm the worst dancer or not the best singer, I'm going to act like the best dancer and best singer. I

think that's what I found in Sharpay. She doesn't really care what people think of her. She thinks she is the best, which is kind of what made the producers want me."

Corbin Bleu, co-star of Discovery Kids' drama *Flight 29 Down* and appearing in the 2007 Disney film *Jump In!* and who would round out the cast of the six main characters, explains that his audition was a long, drawn-out process that took place at the very end of *HSM*'s casting when he auditioned for the role of Ryan Evans. Feeling that he didn't have the right movements for Ryan, the producers suggested that he try out for the role of Chad Danforth.

"I ended up going in for that role and they loved me," he enthuses. "I went through the scene and everything and then they said, 'That was great. Now we're going to bring you back in and we want you to sing.' So I sang something and they said, 'Okay. We love you. That was great. We just have one more thing: you need to come meet the director and sing for him.' So I go meet the director and sing for him. 'Okay. We love you, but we need to watch you play basketball.' So they bring me to a dance studio and I went with the choreographer, Chuck Klapow, and we did basketball as well as dancing. And from there I guess I had one more thing where I actually got to go in with Monique and we read the scene together. From that point I ended up getting it. I think I found out I got the role on Friday and they said, 'Okay, you're flying to Utah on Monday.'"

With Zac, Vanessa, Ashley, Lucas, Monique and Corbin cast, Borden was thrilled. "The kids were amazing," he opines. "The great thing about a musical is, if you don't have talent, you can't be in it. There's no faking it."

As the rest of the world would soon discover, this six-pack of actors had talent to spare.

MEET THE STARS OF
High School Musical

You love to sing along with the songs and to try and match the dance steps of the characters who make up the student body of East High in *High School Musical*, but who are the people behind the characters? Obviously from watching the film we know all about Troy Bolton, Gabriella Montez, Sharpay Evans, Chad Danforth, Taylor McKessie and Ryan Evans, but what about their real-life alter egos?

In the following in-depth profiles you'll learn all you could possibly want to know about those amazing actors and actresses: Zac Efron, Vanessa Anne Hudgens, Ashley Tisdale, Corbin Bleu, Monique Coleman and Lucas Grabeel. From the early days of their careers, through their struggles to break into the business, to being cast in *HSM* and beyond into new projects, it's all here.

ZAC EFRON
Troy Bolton

Although Zac Efron was definitely out there hustling for roles over the course of several years, it's undoubtedly his role as Troy Bolton in the Disney Channel's *High School Musical* that has turned him (as well as his co-stars from that film) into a household name. And now it looks like Zac is in for even bigger and better things as he stars in the film version of the Broadway musical *Hairspray* and reprises his role of Troy in Disney's *High School Musical 2*, both reaching fans in 2007.

Zac was born on October 18, 1987, to parents Starla Baskett and David Efron. For most of his life, he lived in San Luis Obispo, California. As he has explained it, both of his parents moved there approximately 20 years ago and both ended up employed at the same

Zac has often been told that when he was younger, his father noticed that any time a song came on the radio, Zac would start to sing along with it and that he could actually carry a tune. His dad was amazed that his son seemed to have a natural talent for singing, which was something that no one else in the family had ever demonstrated.

"I was actually forced by my dad into my first musical," Zac admits. "I was not very good at all the sports. I was really small when I was younger. I was pretty bad at Little League baseball. I think I scored two points my entire basketball season. So my dad convinced me to go out and audition for my first play. I said, 'Yes,' thinking it was

power plant, his mom working as a secretary for his dad's boss. Starla and David felt a pretty strong connection with each other and, as Zac has often said, "one thing led to another," they fell in love and eventually Zac was brought into the world — joined on February 6, 1992, by little brother Dylan.

Early on, Zac seemed pretty much like any other kid and was interested in the same things as any average little boy. Acting, or even the idea of performing was not something that had occurred to him, though he has said he did enjoy being creative. Sports were also a part of his life — or at least he wanted them to be a part of his life. Unfortunately, he didn't quite have the aptitude that he desired. Not that he didn't give it his best — he tried the whole Little League thing, but kind of struck out. Then he moved on to basketball, but didn't fare much better. As a result, there was a chance that he could have just drifted around without any real direction, until his father intervened. Instead of continuing to push the idea of sports, as many would have, he encouraged him to give acting a try.

Zac with his mother Starla on the set of WB's *Summerland*.

into this audition," he recalls, "but I went in and got the part. And then it was onwards and upwards."

So profound was the effect of the theater on his life that he highly recommends it for anyone attempting a career in acting. "Doing a play has worked for so many people," he says. "There is a magical feeling of learning and the energy is intense. It's so nice to be in front of an audience and receive their energy; it really sparks your passion. There is no better way to learn skills — go out and try theater. Local theater is everywhere."

Zac appeared in a number of regional productions, among them *Mame, Peter Pan, The Music Man* and *Little Shop of Horrors.* During all of this, he was slowly being filled with the desire to start acting in front of the camera, whether it be for film or television. He emphasizes that it wasn't always easy, particularly the process of going out for auditions. "It's ruthless," he states. "There are several thousand kids out there with brown hair and blue eyes who are my age trying to be in movies. Getting a job is like beating a casino. For every role that I have done on TV and movies, I've auditioned for 30 or 40."

in a few months and that somehow I would talk myself out of it by then. Little did I know it was, like, the next day. So I went into this situation kicking and screaming, and little did I know my dad had just shown me the coolest thing on earth at the time. He opened so many doors for me. I auditioned for every single play that was in our area. Luckily, I booked some of the roles and started doing very well."

His first role was in the musical *Gypsy*; he played Newsboy Number One. "It was a very small part, but I was still terrified going

The auditions started to pay off for him in 2002, as things slowly came together as he scored a guest-starring role in the FOX sci-fi series *Firefly* (created by *Buffy the Vampire Slayer*'s Joss Whedon), followed in rapid succession by roles on *ER, The Guardian,* the pilots *The Big Wide World of Carl Laemke* and *Triple Play, CSI: Miami, Navy NCIS* and *Heist.* It's extremely likely that fans of *High School Musical* first became familiar with Zac from his guest-starring appearance on the hit Disney Channel series *The Suite Life of Zack & Cody*, which represented the first time he had a chance to work with *HSM* co-star Ashley Tisdale. In the film they were "enemies," whereas on *The Suite Life* they became romantically involved.

Before *Zack & Cody*, however, he definitely had the opportunity to make a strong impression on the television audience when he was cast on the WB's prime-time soap *Summerland* in the role of Cameron Bale.

"I went in to audition," he explains, "and two weeks later they gave me a role, and this was just a guest-starring role and this was after only one audition. Before *Summerland*, everything I had done was just a guest-starring role and you don't really get to know the cast when you're there for just a day or two. Then when *Summerland* came along, I was a guest star at the time, but slowly I became a part of the cast. Everything is completely different when you're around people like that. They're like your family. And when you get to know everybody, it's more like hanging around with a bunch of friends. It's much more relaxed."

Zac was so good in his guest-starring role that he quickly became a recurring character and in the show's second (and final) season was a series regular, which was particularly exciting for him. "I really got to see what acting is like," he says. "I think it was a great way to break into the business. Like I said, I got to build a family with the people at *Summerland*."

He notes that he would see his co-stars at least three days a week, and that there was something of a strange feeling that came over him; a feeling he believes comes with appearing on a TV series as a regular as opposed to a guest star. As a result, he was able to get a real grasp of what seemed to be a different type of work environment.

During his *Summerland* stint, Zac also starred in the Lifetime TV movie *Miracle Run*, playing an autistic teenager named Steven Morgan, who is encouraged by his mother to participate in a special race and prove that he can be more than people are expecting him to be. "I was so happy to get the role," he admits. "I came in at the last

minute and right after I did the audition, I got the call and they asked me to do the movie. Within the next day or two, I flew out and began shooting in Louisiana and it was amazing."

In between all the guest spots, he also managed to star in *The Derby Stallion*, an equestrian drama originally designed to be released in theaters, but which seems more likely go straight to DVD instead. In that film, he plays Patrick McCardle, a teen who befriends the elderly Mr. Jones and ultimately finds himself involved in a horse race that means a great deal to Mr. Jones — and the film ended up meaning a great deal to Zac.

"I assumed when I signed on for this movie that it was all going to be done by stuntmen," he says. "Then the first day when I came on the set and I talked to one of our producers, he said, 'Yes, you have three lessons and you're going to be jumping!' I guess that really turned on my adrenaline. I started focusing 24/7 on horseback riding."

Then, of course, came the biggest break of all with *High School Musical*, in which he was cast as basketball jock Troy Bolton. "The whole experience was amazing," enthuses Zac. "It was a dream to have one project where I could sing, dance, play basketball and act — all in just six weeks. I got thrown into the mix and immediately I was off and running and practicing constantly for this role. We had so much fun. I have to admit, I'm not much of a dancer, so it took a lot of Gatorade and aspirin to get me through dancing and basketball rehearsals."

"I have to admit, I'm not much of a dancer, so it took a lot of Gatorade and aspirin to get me through dancing and basketball rehearsals."

The real question, of course, was whether or not all of that preparation was worth it in the end, though one can just imagine the answer considering the phenomenon *High School Musical* has become.

"Going into the production, you could tell there was a lot of momentum behind the movie," he offers. "Everyone was very enthusiastic while we made the film, which is uncharacteristic of a lot of movies. The cast and crew were very excited the whole time we were making it, and that came through on camera. I hoped it would do as well as it's done. I'm ecstatic."

His biggest challenge might be playing Link Larkin in *Hairspray*, a very different kind of musical, which originated from the mind of the eccentric John Waters as a film nearly 20 years ago. For the film, Zac dyed his hair black and gained 15 pounds, but then had to transform himself back in time for *High School Musical 2*. Still, as he's proven throughout his career, Zac is up for any challenge put before him.

VANESSA ANNE HUDGENS
Gabriella Montez

Like so many of her celebrity peers, Vanessa Anne Hudgens' talent as a performer was discovered in the family living room. Okay, that might be a slight exaggeration, but the truth is that before she was 10, Vanessa had spent considerable time singing and acting in front of family and friends, and conveyed genuine talent to anyone who watched her.

One could say that on December 14, 1988, Vanessa was born into the family business . . . in a sense. Her parents are Greg Hudgens and Gina Guangco (who between them come from Irish, Native American, Filipino, Chinese and Spanish descent), and all four of her grandparents were musicians during the big-band era.

When Vanessa was eight, she auditioned for and was cast in a number of locally staged musicals, among them *Evita*, *The Wizard of Oz*, *The King and I*, *Carousel*, *Cinderella*, *Damn Yankees* and *The Music Man*. Her life was literally changed when a friend who couldn't make a commercial audition asked her to step in and she did — to great success. Scoring the commercial, Vanessa was on her way, and shortly thereafter her family made the move from Salinas, California, to Los Angeles. She does point out that moving was nothing new to her as the Hudgens family did quite a bit of relocating when she was younger — which made it tough to establish and maintain close friendships.

"I personally have moved a lot in my life, so I don't really have much in the way of friends," she explains. "Because I keep moving, it's hard for me to keep friends and just live a normal life. My best friend is actually Ashley Tisdale, and she's in the business with me and in *High School Musical* with me. My family are the ones who will always be there for me, whereas some friends come and they go, but now and then you find a really loyal friend. All of my friends are pretty much older than me or in the business, so we all understand each other. I haven't been to real school since I was in seventh grade, so I don't know very many people out of the business. My old school is 50 miles from where I live now, so my close friends that I have there, I have to drive a long way to see. The people I do hang out with, I really trust and they are always there for me.

Vanessa Anne Hudgens at the *Thunderbirds* premiere in Los Angeles, July 2004

"But it's a choice that I made," she continues. "A part of me misses regular school, because I am a teenager and when I was a little kid, I always dreamed of going to the prom. A part of me wants to do that, but I know my full heart wants to do acting, so I gave that up. I am still doing schooling, just at home."

"Being cool is being your own self, not doing something that someone else is telling you to do.".

Once in L.A., Vanessa began auditioning for film and television, and in 2002 scored a guest-starring appearance on the CBS sitcom *Still Standing*, playing a character named Tiffany in the episode "Still Rocking." That same year she also landed a more dramatic role as a 10-year-old version of the character Nicole in the "Had" episode of that same network's *Robbery Homicide Division*. In 2003 she played Lindsey in the "New Tunes" episode of *The Brothers Garcia*. More importantly, she played the supporting role of Noel in the critically acclaimed dramatic film *Thirteen*, which followed a pair of teenagers on a road of self-destruction. In a lot of ways, *Thirteen* was eye-opening for Vanessa, alerting her to certain things going on in the real world that she was oblivious to.

"It was a controversial film," she points out. "It was basically about wild teenagers who make the wrong decisions and take the wrong path."

When kids are young, Vanessa explains, they want to experience a wide variety of things, but they often don't recognize the downside of what they're doing before it's too late.

"I really think that people need to be educated about things like drugs and alcohol and what they can do to you in the long term. You just shouldn't do it and it's not something that's very beneficial to you in the first place. Go out and shop if that makes you feel better, rather than doing something stupid or that you're pressured into doing. Peer pressure is always a big thing. I know everyone says that, but it's definitely one of the biggest things. Being cool is being your own self, not doing something that someone else is telling you to do." This theme, of course, would also be at the heart of *High School Musical*, though far less seriously than in *Thirteen*.

Her next role was in the science-fiction film *Thunderbirds*, which was based on the 1960s children's series of the same name and was directed by *Star Trek*'s Jonathan Frakes.

"My best friend is actually Ashley Tisdale, and she's in the business with me and in *High School Musical* with me."

Vanessa played the character Tintin, and was thrilled to have the opportunity to take on a leading role. Unfortunately the film didn't fare that well at the box office.

Vanessa was introduced to the tween audience with guest appearances on *Drake & Josh* and on the Disney Channel's *The Suite Life of Zack & Cody*, in which she appeared as Corrie, a classmate of Maddie (Ashley Tisdale) and London (Brenda Song). Of *The Suite Life* she says, "It was so much fun, because I'm really good friends with Brenda Song too, and Cole and Dylan [Sprouse] are so adorable. I knew them from before, because I used to visit the set all the time. We just had a blast. And Monique Coleman's been on it too, and Zac."

Next up for her was *High School Musical*. The success of that film, of course, paved the way for her to launch her solo music career before she reprises the role of Gabriella Montez in *High School Musical 2*. Let's face it, as far as Vanessa and her co-stars are concerned, *HSM* is the gift that keeps on giving.

ASHLEY TISDALE
Sharpay Evans

Actress Ashley Tisdale is in the enviable position of having a giant fan base for not just one character she plays, but two, and these characters are pretty much diametrically opposed. On one side is her portrayal of "good girl" Maddie on the Disney Channel's *The Suite Life of Zack & Cody*, and on the other is the self-important, manipulative Sharpay Evans from *High School Musical*.

Born on July 2, 1985, to parents Mike and Lisa Tisdale, Ashley's career actually began when she was only three years old and was discovered by manager Bill Perlman (a position he still holds today) as she and her mom shopped at a New Jersey mall. Although Lisa was reluctant to get Ashley involved in the entertainment world — her brother had been a model — she ultimately acquiesced, saying that Ashley could try out for one commercial.

"It was a national commercial for J.C. Penney," Ashley recalls. "The fact that I had really curly dark hair, kind of like Shirley Temple, and was kind of different from everybody else, I went in there and booked it. Then I booked seven national commercials consecutively after that."

When she turned eight, after years of acting in commercials and modeling for print publications, Ashley announced that she wanted to audition for the touring company of Broadway's *Les Miserables*. She had seen the musical and fallen in love with it, and when she saw *Party of Five*'s Lacy Chabert — who she knew from commercial auditions — perform as Cosette, it was inspiring. Naturally her parents and manager were a bit skeptical, particularly considering how many people would be in the audience and the fact that, as a child, she was somewhat shy — plus she had never sung in public before.

"I'd never had a singing lesson in my life," she details. "I just had two singing lessons for the actual audition and then I booked it. That first night, my dad recalls that

I was so nervous. I was sitting there and my legs were quivering, but of course when you're on stage and all of the lights are off, you can't really see anything except for the exit signs, so that wasn't really that bad. That kind of helped me overcome the fear of being in front of the audience. Acting was a way for me to express myself and come

Ashley Tisdale in her earlier, curlier days, in October 2003.

out of my shell and not be so quiet and shy. I love performing now and can't wait to be on a stage in front of an audience."

Ashley was performing as Cosette in *Les Miserables* for about a year and a half when her parents thought that that was a long enough time to be "on the road." She, of course, had other ideas, and wanted to audition for the title role in the international tour of *Annie*, which she was hired for. As a result, she spent four weeks with the show in Korea before coming home. Lisa and Mike wanted her to return to something resembling a normal life, but, having visited Pasadena, California, while part of *Les Mis*, Ashley definitely had other ideas.

"I wanted to go there to do TV shows," she states. "That's when we started to go back and forth between California and New Jersey. My first show was *Smart Guy*, which was from the same creator and producer as *Suite Life*. They gave me my first job ever in California, which was awesome."

A role in *Ask Harriet* secured her a "holding deal" at Columbia Tri-Star, which kept her at the studio throughout pilot season of that year, though *Harriet* ultimately didn't go to series. Still, her seemingly instant success convinced the family that moving to California wasn't a bad idea, so mom, dad and sister Jennifer all uprooted themselves and went west.

Ashley scored a number of guest-starring roles in such shows as *7th Heaven, Grounded For Life, Boston Public, Strong Medicine, Charmed* and *Beverly Hills 90210*. She was also a recurring role on the series *The Hughleys* and *Still Standing*, and managed to score a small role in the feature film *Donnie Darko*.

Ashley in November 2004, before she lightened her hair color to appear in *The Suite Life of Zack & Cody.*

Ashley with her sister, Jennifer, who is also an actress.

Yet despite it all Ashley managed to maintain a normal life — thanks to the fact that her parents insisted that she attend a regular school and have a normal job, working at clothing stores in the mall.

"They wanted me to understand how hard it was to work on top of what I was doing," Ashley details. "It was definitely good, but at the time I didn't like it. I hated it, actually. I was, like, 'I would rather be shopping than putting away all the go-backs.' But when I look back at it from where I am today, it's made me totally grateful and I won't take it for granted. I'm so happy that I've had that life and been able to experience a normal life besides this,

> " I figure when I'm 30 or 40 I can play those edgy parts, because my fan base will have grown up with me."

because it's something to draw experiences from. So I've had a normal life, but I *have* struggled to get here. It hasn't been handed to me and it hasn't been easy."

All of Ashley's efforts came to fruition when she auditioned for and was cast as Maddie in *The Suite Life of Zack & Cody*, a role that tapped in to her dreams of being a Lucille Ball–type of character, doing physical comedy.

The series stars Dylan and Cole Sprouse as the sons of the headlining singer at Boston's Tipton Hotel, who actually live at the Tipton. Brenda Song plays the owner's spoiled daughter, London; while Ashley is Maddie, the counter girl and sometimes babysitter to Zack and Cody.

"It's a fun show because the kids actually get to star in it," she enthuses. "In a network sitcom at the time, the role of a young kid would be very minimal. I'm also excited because the show is taped in front of an audience and because I come from stage and the theater, this kind of reminds me of that. I love doing comedy in front of an audience and getting the rush of energy that

provides. What's nice is that when you mess up and stuff, it's not a huge thing. With theater you have to keep on going no matter what, whereas if you mess up on the show you can redo the scene. You can have fun with it and entertain the audience while you're redoing it. The best part is that they love when you mess up; they think it's hysterical. But it's very similar [to theater] and that's why I really enjoy it and love it."

Thanks to her success on *The Suite Life of Zack & Cody* and then in *High School Musical*, Ashley's star at Disney has definitely risen, much as Hilary Duff's and Lindsay Lohan's did before her. Is she concerned she'll be locked into a certain kind of role, or fearful of a backlash when she tries to break free from the Disney image?

"Right now," she says, "I'm very comfortable with where I am. One of the things that makes me different from those girls is that I'm older playing younger. I'm much older and I'm on Disney. I like playing younger because I look younger and I am pretty young for my age. So it's a comfortable situation, because I wouldn't want to audition for 20-year-old parts, first because I wouldn't get them and, then, because I wouldn't be comfortable playing them. With some other actors, they want to be older, they want to play older and they don't want that audience. But I do. I figure when I'm 30 or 40 I can play those edgy parts, because my fan base will have grown up with me. So right now I'm not worried at all, and when the time is right I will play those parts. It's hard to make that transition and I think that's what a lot of people are

Ashley with Brenda Song, who co-stars as London on *The Suite Life of Zack & Cody*.

going through. Some people do it really fast and don't take their time doing it, but that's not where I stand. I think where I'm very mature is in terms of my goals."

Speaking of maturing, she believes that Maddie has grown and evolved through the course of *The Suite Life*. "She's definitely more developed as a character," Ashley muses. "In the beginning, she and London did not get along whatsoever, but through-

out the show you see that the reason for it is that they have such different lifestyles. Maddie comes to understand where [London's] coming from, so Maddie has definitely changed. There's no end to story-lines in a hotel and that's a lot of fun, and the character just being the babysitter and candy counter girl and the girl next door, she gets in these totally different situations. In the Jesse McCartney episode, she and

London had to dress up as men, which was really funny. In one episode, she's a Russian masseuse trying to catch a thief. There's always something funny going on, but there's a reason behind it and there's always kind of a message at the end of the episode."

Being on the show allowed Ashley to work with a number of people who appeared as guest stars before co-starring with them in *High School Musical*. "Of course I knew Zac and it's so much fun to have him and people like Vanessa and Monique on the show," she says, "But Jesse McCartney was like a big guest star. We were so excited because 'Beautiful Soul' was so popular, and the fact that he was singing on the show was like you get your own little concert, so there are definitely perks."

Following the release of her first solo album, Ashley reprises her role of Sharpay in *High School Musical 2* and from there . . . whatever direction she goes in, it will undoubtedly be Ashley Tisdale's decision all the way. As it always has been.

CORBIN BLEU
Chad Danforth

Like his castmates from *High School Musical*, Corbin Bleu's career is growing by leaps and bounds with each passing day. Not only has he recorded his first solo album, but he's starred in the Disney Channel original movie *Jump In!* — about a boxer who has a special talent for jumping rope (!) — and of course returns to his *HSM* role of Chad Danforth in the all-new sequel. Not bad for a guy from Brooklyn, New York.

Born on February 21, 1989, Corbin got an early start to his career, being discovered and hired for a print ad at the ripe old age of two, and continued from there, believing that a career in show business was something he was definitely destined for. "As a little kid," he says, "I would constantly memorize lines to movies and repeat them and act them out. That's when my parents were, like, 'We've got to get him into this.'"

51

Corbin with his father, mother, and sister.

And that's precisely what they did. Corbin continued to work as a model and even began to shine as a dancer. From there he decided to give acting a try and it began paying off almost immediately. On the big screen he appeared in the feature films *Soldier* (1998), *Galaxy Quest* and *Mystery Men* (both 1999), *Family Tree* (2000), and *Catch That Kid* (2004). But it was on television where he really began to make his mark and connect with the audience. He appeared in the pilot episode of the Disney Channel's *Hannah Montana* and, of course, in *High School Musical.*

At about the same time that *HSM* was exploding, Corbin was a series regular on the Discovery Kids television series *Flight 29 Down,* which was about how a group of teenagers work together to survive when their plane crashes on an island. In describing his character, Corbin says that Nathan is a former Boy Scout who ends up stranded on

"I am a very open, social, friendly person, and when it comes to people approaching me and asking for an autograph, I am totally cool with doing any of that. It's a lot of fun."

the island with fellow students from prep school. Because he got a lot of attention from his family and knows a bit about survival techniques thanks to his Boy Scout training, he views himself as something of a leader.

"From the beginning," Corbin explains, "Nathan tries to prove to himself and the rest of the group that he can take charge. But he soon finds out that his skills, in reality, aren't that sharp. He persists, however, when all he really needs to do is learn how to be a team player and work with the others. You can't lead a team unless you have a team to lead."

Probably the greatest highlight for him about the show was the opportunity he had to shoot on location in Hawaii and bond with his castmates.

"The island's beauty and serenity are things that can't be imagined unless you experience them for yourself," he reflects. "Hawaii is a really beautiful and relaxing place. We had the beach. We had the stars at

night. The condo we were staying at was two blocks from the beach. It had a patio roof. We'd go up there every night to watch the sunset and the stars. And we shot the show on the beach."

The condo the cast lived in had 12 rooms, allowing everyone to have their own space. "One of the things about us getting along so well," he said of his *Flight 29 Down* cast, "is that we can live close to each other without driving each other crazy. The bonding we got from that was amazing. We saw each other every day at work, and then we'd come home and hang out after work. We had a great time. The condo got a little cramped sometimes, but it was cozy and had a great view."

As enjoyable as the series was, it obviously couldn't compare to the experience of shooting *High School Musical* or to its success and the impact it's had on his life. "*High School Musical* was awesome," he enthuses. "I'd never done a musical movie before, and that was so much fun to do. It's not every day you get the opportunity to do a musical, and I do have a theater background, so it was fun to put that on film. I've been studying dance since I was two years old and I've also been working on my singing. So being able to showcase my skills let me know that all my hard work is paying off.

"One thing about the Disney Channel," Corbin continues, "is that they publicize their products a lot. So with *High School Musical*, I have gotten a lot of publicity, and that publicity has allowed a lot more people to know who I am. And that goes for fans too. When it comes to fans approaching me,

it's happened a lot more since the film aired. But I'm actually a person who loves it. I love people, and it shows that there is an appreciation for my work. I am a very open, social, friendly person, and when it comes to people approaching me and asking for an autograph, I am totally cool with doing any of that. It's a lot of fun."

MONIQUE COLEMAN
Taylor McKessie

In the fall of 2006, ABC launched its third season of *Dancing with the Stars,* and one of the participants was *High School Musical*'s Monique Coleman, better known as Taylor McKessie. In week two, fans were delighted to watch Monique do her thing to the tune of "Bop to the Top."

"I just felt like I needed to bring something that was very close to me to the table," she revealed in an online interview. "And

having Lucas and Ashley and Corbin there to support me just reminded me that no matter what happened on the show or ever, that I have not only walked away knowing some of the most talented people, but that those people are also my friends."

Monique was born on November 13, 1980, in Orangeburg, South Carolina. She began acting in theater and television at "a very young age," according to her official

biography, with early training coming from the Workshop Theater School of Dramatic Arts, where she performed in over 15 plays. An acting class taught by a guest teacher actually turned out to be an audition, and resulted in her booking her first commercial. Getting her first taste of "the business," she began auditioning as much as she possibly could in the Southeast region. This resulted in her scoring several local and regional commercials. She managed to land her first lead role in *Mother of the River*, an independent feature film that was shot in Charleston, South Carolina, and went on to win numerous film festival awards in Chicago.

In 1997 she appeared as "Young Donna" in the Family Channel movie *The Ditchdigger's Daughter*, which resulted in her being nominated for a Young Artists Award of Hollywood. Taking control of things, in her sophomore year of high school, Monique wrote, directed, produced and starred in her own one-person play titled *Voices From Within*. The play was a

major hit; it touched its audience and was a personal accomplishment for the young performer.

Once she was finished with her education, Monique made the move to California to further her career. "When I got to Los Angeles," she explained, "I actually felt a little bit behind, because I was a little bit older than some of the people who were auditioning for the same roles as me because of how young I look. That kind of put me in a category with people who were significantly younger, and I felt like it was sort of a disadvantage. At the same time, school and education were so important to me that I felt that as long as I can break in eventually, then hopefully the skills that I learned in school will help me to maintain a career."

It was a philosophy that definitely paid off for her as she began getting hired as a guest star on a number of different television series, including *Malcolm in the Middle, Strong Medicine, 10-8* and *Veronica Mars*, while scoring recurring roles on *Gilmore Girls, Boston Public* and the Disney Channel series *The Suite Life of Zack & Cody*. In 2005, she starred opposite the legendary James Earl Jones in the Hallmark Movie *The Reading Room*, for which she received a 2006 Camie Award for her portrayal of Leesha, and she represented the film at the NAACP Image Awards, where it was nominated for Outstanding TV Movie, Miniseries or Dramatic Special.

Next up was *High School Musical*, the success of which she never expected. "It's definitely the best thing that's happened to my career and I walked away with great

friends from it," Monique enthuses. "Coming into it, I think everyone was kind of skeptical, because Disney Channel puts out a lot of movies and none of them have been as successful as *High School Musical*. It was a life-changing experience. It really felt like not only a launch pad, but also a training ground as well for how to be on the business side of the industry."

This was followed by the *Dancing with the Stars* gig, which Monique openly admits she was not the first choice for; two of her *HSM* co-stars were offered a shot first, but both turned the show down due to previous professional obligations.

"I talked to one of them," Monique relates, "and they said, 'Maybe you should call them, because I think that you'd be great.' I really had the support of my cast behind me, pushing me to do it. And I love the show so much and have watched every season and have been a huge fan, but never put myself in the mindset that I was even considered a celebrity. And I don't think they [the producers] thought of me because I didn't have such a significant role in the film as a singer/dancer. I really was passionate about that project [*Dancing with the Stars*]. I was the one who was, like, 'I would love to do that.' And then I realized that *High School Musical* was big enough that I *could* approach them on it and I did.

"I fought for it," she adds. "I'm just grateful that they believed in me. I really do feel like they gave me a chance. They took a risk by putting me on this show, and that's part of the reason why I went out there week after week and did my very best. I'm honored by the fact that they were willing to consider me a celebrity and put me on the show."

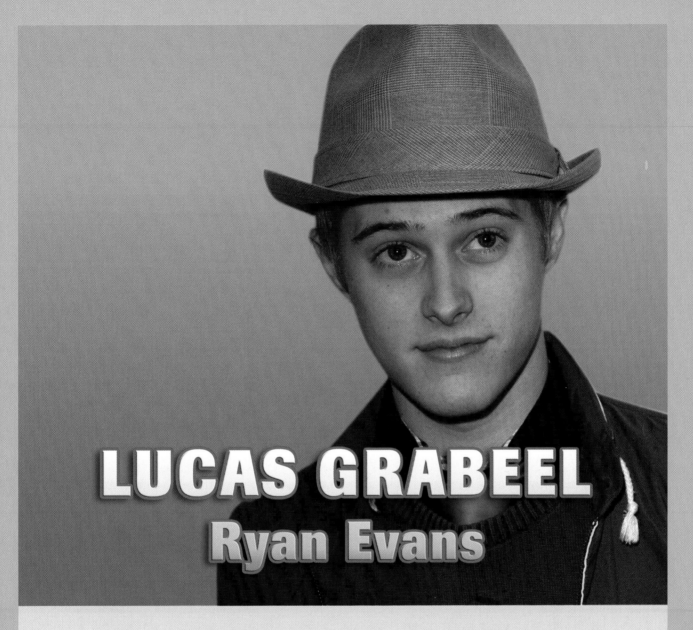

LUCAS GRABEEL
Ryan Evans

Lucas Stephen Grabeel was born on November 23, 1984, in Springfield, Missouri, to Stephen and Jean Grabeel, and immediately became little brother to older sister Autumn.

Like many entertainers, his love for performing became apparent to everyone around him when he was at a young age. It began with him and Autumn creating songs, plays or commercials and acting them out for their family and friends. He *really* fell in love with acting when he was cast in the role of Colin in his high school's production of *The Secret Garden*.

Immediately thereafter he began looking for bigger and better things, and turned his attention to community theater, scoring the role of the Artful Dodger in the Springfield Little Theater's production of *Oliver*. The stage captured his imagination and he remained

there and performed in a total of eight different productions by the time he graduated high school.

He was a member of the theater's young performing troupe for five years, and while there, taught a variety of classes in theater, among them dance, acting and improvisation. His students were of all different ages.

Lucas also played leading roles in his high school's musicals, productions and operas, and participated in music contests and the speech and debate teams. He played drums for the local church, initiated a men's *a cappella* singing group at Kickapoo High School, and attended the Missouri Fine Arts Academy.

As he graduated high school in 2003, Lucas had a decision to make: college or a career. "Once I graduated high school," he says, "I packed my car and moved out to L.A. I skipped college completely and decided to concentrate on my acting. I took the biggest risk I've ever taken in my life, to just pick up and move. But this is what I've always wanted to do. My feeling is that no matter what age you are, the most important thing is to get experience. The teachers can teach you, but try to audition for a play or a performing troupe. Further your knowledge and get smarter. A lot of people think that actors don't have to be smart, but I say read a lot, because knowledge is power. I also have to say that you need to be very focused if you want to succeed in this business."

Once Lucas got to California, things began happening quickly for him. He met his manager, Robert C. Thompson, while standing in line for a smoothie, and within a week he had his agent. Three weeks after that, he managed to line up his first commercial. Within nine months he scored a Disney Channel TV movie, *Halloweentown*

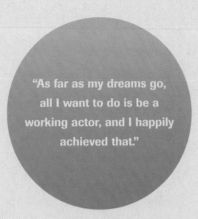

High, which eventually led to his auditioning for *High School Musical* and being cast in the role of Ryan Evans. After the amazing experience of shooting that film, he began making episodic TV appearances on such shows as *Boston Legal, Veronica Mars, 'Til Death* and *Smallville*. Then it was back to Disney for *Return to Halloweentown* and on to the feature film *Alice*, which is based on the book series by Phyllis Reynolds Naylor. After that, to East High with *HSM 2*.

"When I came out to L.A. three years ago," he reflects, "I thought it would be three years to get a job. I never planned in my head that everything was going to happen so fast. I also think it's amazing that I'm singing [as part of *High School Musical*]. Singing is what got me into acting, and I thought once I moved to Los Angeles that wouldn't be a part of my life anymore. But then here it goes — it's just out of nowhere and I had no idea [*HSM*] was going to have this much success.

"Now it is kind of a challenge for me to set new goals every day," he adds, "but my personal goal is also a career goal, and that is to continually ask questions and reach the point where I feel completely comfortable and immersed in the industry. One of the things I was taught was to always ask questions. In the film industry, there are so many sides to the industry — I would love to produce something and be a part of a whole project from beginning to end and see how a film is created from a behind-the-scenes point of view. As far as my dreams go, all I want to do is be a working actor, and I happily achieved that."

TWO SIDES OF A COIN
The Cast Meets Their Characters

The cast had to very quickly become acquainted with their *High School Musical* characters, getting a feel for who they were and what their motivations were before filming could get underway.

"Troy is a cool guy, super jock extraordinaire," says Zac, "and, boy, I wish I was more like my character. He's the big shot on campus and normally you think of that guy in a negative light, but Troy is the opposite. He's a nice guy; but he balances [being popular] by not giving into peer pressure or being a jerk to people. Personally, I was never the cool kid. I was always sort of a bookworm. I would just like to be more like Troy, because he's so cool. And he's so good at basketball. He gets all the cool girls. He's like the dream character to play. I think that every guy would like being more like Troy when they were in high school.

"I have to say that I was sort of in the same boat as Troy when I was hanging out at school," he adds. "All my extracurricular activities were involved with performing — singing and dancing and theater. Reactions were mixed. Everyone thought it was so cool to be a part of the basketball team, but to go out and be in places like the local theater houses wasn't that

> "My character is a little bit brighter in the math and science department than I am . . . okay, a lot."
> — Monique Coleman

65

cool, I guess. But it would be really fun to have your friends come and watch the shows, because then they could see what the heck you're doing all this time when you're missing school and aren't able to hang out. One of the things that I had to overcome, like Troy does, is peer pressure. Just like in *High School Musical*, it was against theater and I just tried to follow what I really wanted to do."

As for Gabriella, Vanessa explains, "She's kind of the brainy girl who just likes to cuddle up with a good book. I like playing the role because it's nice to show that the brainy girls can also be pretty. Usually when brainy girls are shown in films, they kind of are presented as nerds or someone not very social. I think Gabriella and Taylor [McKessie] break out of that. We show that it's okay to be smart. Both my character and I fight for what we want. Personally, I would rather go out and go to the movies with my friends or just hang out with them, whereas I think Gabriella likes to stay at home by the fire."

Ashley sees Sharpay as "the drama queen. She rules the school, mainly the villain, gets thrown by Troy and Gabriella for wanting to go out for a musical. I'm nothing like her, thank God. But I probably can relate to her, because of her passion for performing. I love to perform, so that's probably the most similar thing I have to her. I watched a lot of movies to prepare for playing her. I actually watched *Mean Girls* with Rachel McAdams and I liked how she portrayed her character. She was a mean girl, but she had a smile on her face whenever she did it. So I watched all these other things and kind of put some things in and made it creative myself. I just loved playing the mean girl. When you're not like a character, it's kind of fun to play."

Lucas expresses his sincere hope that he and Ryan are nothing alike. "I am a simple, plain person," he says "You know, I'm chilled and laid back and not so out there and crazy."

In describing Taylor, Monique says, "She is the president of the chemistry club and the head of the scholastic decathlon, as well as best friends with Gabriella. And my character is a little bit brighter in the math and science department than I am . . . okay, a lot. I did really well in English and more creative subjects. But I definitely share her zest for education; I think it's really important for girls to know that it's cool to be smart. And I think that's something I really share [with Taylor]."

Corbin believes that his character, Chad, is probably most similar to Taylor in terms of attitude. "He is the equivalent to Monique's character," Corbin explains. "He's the best friend of Troy Bolton, who is a basketball jock. It's something he's been doing his whole life. He's very, very into basketball. I guess he's sort of the antagonist in the fact that he tries to stop Troy from doing his singing thing. I'm similar to Chad in the way that he has a strong passion for what he

does. He's very into it with the full force of what he does, but at the same time I'm kind of sports-challenged. You know, you give me a ball and I don't know what to do with this thing. I'm very athletic, it's just when it comes to different sports and things I'm not used to. But I also work really hard at what I do. As you can see, in the end I was very comfortable with the ball. It's just something that once I get used to it, I just kind of take it with me and I go and run with it."

He elaborates, offering his opinion on the history between Chad and Troy, musing that their friendship was not established in high school. Instead, it's his belief that they've been friends since kindergarten and elementary school. "They grew up together," he says, "so I think I really just wanted to make Chad as comfortable as possible around Troy, because with certain friends there are certain boundaries you would make if you just met. Chad will totally put Troy in a little headlock and give him a noogie. I wanted him to be as relaxed as possible around Troy, because Troy is family to him."

Ironically, Chad spends much of *High School Musical* trying to convince Troy that he shouldn't be involved in the school musical, but Chad is one of the first to break into song and dance. Laughing, Corbin explains that one of the beauties of a musical movie is that a character has no choice but to dance

"Personally, I was never the cool kid. I was always sort of a bookworm. I would just like to be more like Troy, because he's so cool."
— Zac Efron

for the sake of the movie. "It's great," he says, "because with every number, you end up breaking into song and dance. One of the coolest numbers is 'Get'cha Head in the Game,' which is a basketball dance number. We are actually dancing with basketballs and bouncing basketballs all over the place and putting them through our legs. It starts that we are practicing for a game, and then all of a sudden the ball starts making a beat and the squeak of the shoes start going into it and it goes into this major dance break. It's really cool."

GETTING THEIR HEADS IN THE GAME

There was something about Zac, Vanessa, Ashley, Lucas, Monique and Corbin that appealed to director Kenny Ortega, *High School Musical*'s producers and the Disney executives, but passing the audition was only the beginning for them. This group would have to travel to Salt Lake City, Utah (where filming would take place), and undergo what undoubtedly seemed like the equivalent of Army boot camp in order to get ready for filming.

In Ortega's mind, choreography was a key element, and he would be calling on everything he had learned from his mentor, the late, great actor and dancer Gene Kelly, whom Ortega had worked with on 1980's Olivia Newton John musical fantasy *Xanadu*.

"When I first met him," Ortega reflects, "he realized I had very little knowledge of designing choreography for the camera. He was one of the pioneers of that. He took me under his wing and unselfishly passed down a tremendous amount of creative and technical information to me. I'm forever indebted to him. I think you can see the influence in this

film, which honors his principles and the spirit of enthusiasm and abandon he brought to everything he did."

Ortega, along with fellow choreographers Charles Klapow and Bonnie Story, began working with the cast to teach them the steps to the musical numbers. The sometimes eight-hour-a-day dance rehearsals continued well into the five-week shoot, as the cast — as well as the numerous local extras and dancers that were brought in — expanded their horizons to learn hip-hop, jazz and modern moves for each elaborate production piece. Some of these numbers actually included more than 40 dancers.

According to Zac, there was a bit of mystery surrounding the fact that they were flying to Utah two weeks prior to the beginning of photography on the film. "Little did we know," he laughs, "that they had two solid weeks of intense dancing, acting, singing and basketball rehearsals along with strange stretching and things I'd never heard of before — and then working on acting scenes. It was like boot camp. We'd wake up at six in the morning and work until six

at night. It was incredible. I don't know how I made it through. I can't believe I am still walking. I had so many muscle pulls and shin splints and was so sore, but so much better than I was before. I learned more in those two weeks than I'd learned in the previous years. Every second of it was worth it. Everyone in that movie was a trooper."

Vanessa remembers male cast members ending up with shin splints due to the fact that they had to follow dance rehearsals with basketball practice. "It was so long learning the dance, rehearsals, and learning [more] dances — from the morning to the evening. We would be dancing our little butts away, and even after that, Ashley and I were really trying to get into shape, so we would go to the gym at our hotel. So we would go home after the dancing and work out at the gym."

Laughs Ashley, "Our parents thought we were crazy. They were, like, 'Oh my God, you're going to the gym after dancing for so many hours?' What's funny is Zac sort of became our personal trainer. He was totally into working out."

It's Vanessa's opinion that the most difficult part of those rehearsals probably took place at the beginning of the process, although she does commend Ortega for his

sweetness and the fact that there would be a lot of give and take between the director and his cast.

"*That* was a lot of fun," Vanessa recalls. "The hard part was probably just working it all day. It's tiring, but I just love every part of it, because I grew up in musical theater. I haven't danced in a while, because I have been moving a lot and I haven't found a studio to go to. Just getting back to that was really getting into the groove, but in the beginning, Kenny, Zac and I would just sit down, turn on the music and break free. Zac and I just got up there and kind of just did our own thing, and then Kenny gave us some ideas and it was just such a creative process."

Regarding working with Ortega, Ashley adds, "First of all, Kenny Ortega was a great director and choreographer, and our producers were amazing and they just let us be creative with our characters. We got to think up so many things. Each of us would say, 'Oh, it would be funny if you did that,' and we would call each other with ideas. We were having so much fun and I think it came across on screen."

For Corbin, the dancing lessons that had proven so grueling to his co-stars were relatively easy as he had been dancing his whole life. Making basketball look natural, however, was a different matter. "What was cool," he says, "is that I really worked hard on it and by the end of the last week, I was able to spin a basketball on my finger. That was the hardest part for me. It was funny, because most of the other guys had played basketball. I was probably the weakest [player] out of them. When it came to the dancing part, a lot of them weren't as strong. I was able to help them. It was really cool that we got to feed off each other and help each other."

Ashley admits that she's not the best dancer in the world or the most coordinated, but credits Ortega with whipping her and her co-stars into shape. "You will probably watch me and never guess that I'm not a good dancer, because he just let us portray what we would do with the song and kind of perform our own thing to it, and then he added stuff that he thought was good."

THEY'RE ALL IN THIS TOGETHER

and, inadvertently, develop a tight-knit bond between them.

Explains Vanessa, "We stayed in a hotel, but we all stayed on the same floor relatively close to each other. We just had a blast. We were all hanging out, watching movies, and Ashley and I would go shopping. Like I said, we actually went to the gym, as crazy as that is, after dance rehearsal all day."

"One of the best parts of filming for me was just hanging out with everyone on set," says Zac. "I made so many friends. I knew Ashley beforehand, and she's probably the only one out of the cast that I knew, but it was amazing the relationships we built. We remained best friends coming out of it."

Reflects Corbin, "Once, after having a great day filming and hanging out at dinner, the cast came into the hotel pretty late. We were all still very excited from the day, so to get out the rest of our energy, we performed the dance finale in the middle of the hotel lobby."

Perhaps most exciting to Zac is the fact that he and his co-stars have remained so tight with each other, which, he's discov-

Filming of *High School Musical* took place over the course of 25 days in the summer of 2005 at a real Salt Lake City school. The locale was perfect in that it allowed non-musical sequences to be shot at the same time that song and dance routines were being practiced. More importantly, it moved cast and crew away from the Hollywood scene and into a setting that allowed everyone to focus on the making of the movie

ered, is not normally the case. "We've grown closer *after* filming, and that is a very strange situation," he says, "because usually after a movie ends, the cast loses touch. For instance, I am not in touch with the cast of *Summerland.* We [the *HSM* cast] have grown closer together as all of the press interviews and appearances have gone on."

Monique feels that the group is actually "lucky" that they found each other. "We're really like family and I really get along with everyone. We see a lot of one another. One of the things I am proud of is that we have avoided the tendency to have cliques among us. And we seem to be together a lot. We mainly do press, interviews. We did a junket

for the video premiere at the Four Seasons in Beverly Hills. We were on *TRL, Good Morning America,* cnn's *Showbiz Tonight* and did a lot of tv interviews. And we are always doing teen mag interviews and photo sessions."

In the case of Vanessa and Ashley, they were already friends prior to *High School Musical,* and had acted together as well when Vanessa appeared on Ashley's series, *The Suite Life of Zack & Cody* (which Monique had also appeared on).

"Actually, I originally met her on a commercial we did for Sears, where we were dancing as well, which is funny," Vanessa smiles. "That was probably around two years ago. The first time we saw each other after we knew we had gotten *High School Musical* was in the recording studio. We just ran to each other, screamed and jumped up and down like a pair of little girls. We were just so excited." As to the closeness they've established between each other, she adds, "Ashley's very loyal to me. If we have a problem with each other, we tell each other. We won't let it sit in the back of our minds; we'll actually tell each other that there's something bothering us so our relationship doesn't get hurt. She's just very sweet and so funny and just crazy."

Ashley's *HSM* joy comes from the fact that when the cast got together, everyone seemed determined to just have fun and not allow egos to interfere with anything.

"I think that's the key thing," Ashley muses. "When someone has an ego, they're very hard to work with. Through this whole process, we've kept up with not having that. I have to say, *Suite Life* is such a family over there, and *High School Musical* is a family too, but there's something different about *High School Musical*. There's a magical thing that kind of happened. It sounds kind of cheesy, but anyone you ask from the cast would agree. It's very different when you're away from where you live, because you're constantly with each other. Because the cast was in Utah, we weren't with our normal families; we were always with each other, although part of it is that a lot of us were friends before the film. It was so much fun to go out every night.

"Time has only brought us closer with everything that's been going on," she continues. "We are like brothers and sisters. I can't

explain it, but with the producers and Kenny Ortega, they made the whole atmosphere. They brought us to the planetarium and the aquarium and the movies on weekends, when they didn't have to. Kenny would put together a club night where we would have themes like a dancing night, and he was like a kid himself. We were always together and it was such a blast! That's where all the chemistry came from — being with each other all the time and being able to connect like that on a personal level, which made our characters connect as well.

"When we performed 'We're All in This Together,' that night was the last night for filming for me and when we were doing the number, Kenny just kept saying again and again, 'Connect. Just connect.' We already

Ashley also reflects on the excitement that was building in the cast prior to the film making its debut on the Disney Channel. As she explains it, she, Zac and Vanessa would hang out together in the days before its airing.

"When we were together," she says, "we would put on the music and perform it for our friends at barbecues. We would perform it because we wanted to tell them what it was about and they wanted to know what the experience was like and what the music was like. We had shot it during the summer and were waiting for it to air in January, so we would show them and they really seemed to like it. It was just so exciting for us. In some ways, the experience itself felt like a dream for us, because when we got back home it almost felt like something that hadn't really happened. So it was kind of cool doing that kind of thing leading to its airing."

knew the dance and he told us not to think about the steps, just dance and feel it and we would connect with the audience. And we really believed in what we were doing; it was such a huge thing for us. When we went to do that, you could totally tell and after one take we were crying. There's a special tape put together for us where you can see us crying. We just really felt that moment and it was amazing."

TRACKING THE PHENOMENON

The world's first glimpse of *High School Musical* was back on Thanksgiving 2005 with 15-second teaser spots that ran on the Disney Channel. This was followed in December when music videos from the film aired, and the cast was introduced to the Disney audience on a New Year's Eve special.

On January 9, 2006, two weeks before the Disney Channel premiere of *High School Musical*, Matt Palmer, Senior V.P. of Marketing, gave an interview in which he mentioned, "We're spending double what we normally spend [on marketing for *HSM*], because we see an opportunity to kick off 2006 with a great statement."

That statement began with advertising in such magazines as the now-defunct *Teen People* and promotional spots airing on Radio Disney that were designed to send fans to Disney's Web site. Once there, potential fans would be able to download an MP3 of one of the songs from the soundtrack — with a code picked up from the magazine ad or heard on the radio spot. This was corporate synergy at its most innovative. Additionally, for the premiere, fans could download a *High School Musical* "party kit," so kids could host their own sing-along party, while the second broadcast was paired with a one-time airing of a "making of" documentary.

Disney's Palmer offered, "The whole digital landscape was critical to us. We want to be everywhere kids are. They're the biggest multi-taskers and technology adapters."

On January 10, Disney's Hollywood Records released the soundtrack album to *High School Musical*, which was actually recorded over the course of a week prior to the beginning of shooting. Within a matter of days, it became the #1 album on iTunes and Amazon.com.

Later in the month, word of the impending premiere seemed to be everywhere. Exclaimed Lucas, "Out here we're in the *L.A. Weekly*, we're in *People*, we're in *Pop Star*. At the malls, they have posters up. . . . It's pretty crazy. We're on almost every bus stop out here. Everywhere I go, *High School Musical* is right there." It was only a short matter of time before *High School Musical* was absolutely *everywhere*.

Just before the film debuted, the nation's critics offered their opinon of it, among them:

The Dallas Morning News: "If only real life were as happy as it is in *High School Musical*,

where the scrubbed-faced jocks are talking and dancing with the scrubbed-faced decathlon team members, who are singing with the cheerleaders, who are dancing with the skater kids. Do you feel another song coming on? . . . This is sleepover movie material. This is popcorn and paint-your-toenails girl stuff. It's fun, frivolous and totally vapid. A pillow fight afterward would be totally appropriate."

Daily Variety: "It's doubtful that show-tunes will ever be cool among teens and tweens, but Disney Channel certainly makes a convincing case for the return of the musical with an original pic from *Dirty Dancing*'s Kenny Ortega. Featuring an immensely appealing cast and some highly clever, toe-tapping tunes, *High School Musical* should strike the right chord with Mouse fans."

The Onion: "Mostly, *High School Musical* makes an appealing case for an idealized vision of high school, where individuality is celebrated and even the mean kids know everyone's name."

DVD Talk: "*High School Musical* is fun. Lots of fun. Sure, other Disney Channel movies have been fun too, but this one, well, it's downright electric. The songs are a bit on the generic side of the teen-pop-idol equation, and yet they sizzle, these catchy tunes that are tailor-made to get stuck in your head and keep you humming along; director/choreographer Kenny Ortega (who previously helmed *Newsies* and served as choreographer for *Dirty Dancing*) makes the music jump with big, bouncy dance numbers that are such a delight to watch; and the cast is filled with youngsters who can do the singing and the dancing, yes, but they're also charming as can be. It all adds up to something that simply sparks."

Kids.tvmovies.about.com: "*High School Musical* presents the social concerns kids face in a non-threatening, win-win way. Instead of following the usual tactic of the genre and allowing the underdog to prevail over the evil popular crowd, *High School*

Zac Efron with Paula Abdul.

Musical brings students together and recognizes each person's talent and contribution."

Entertainment Weekly: "The songs are wispy but lively trifles with positive-thinking lyrics including, yes, 'Everyone is special in their own way'…. Nothing here is better than your average high school production of *The Music Man*, but *High School Musical*, with its big throbbing heart, gives out all the right messages without being slow-witted or preachy. Its alternate title could have been *Squeaky-Clean Dancing*."

BBC.com: "If you're a song and dance fan and you love any high school–related plot — this is the movie for you. It's the new *Grease* with a toe-tapping soundtrack and hot new stars. I wish my high school was like this!"

High School Musical debuted on the Disney Channel to an audience of 7.7 million, the highest ever for a cable movie. Between this and six additional broadcasts by the end of February, a total of 28.3 million people tuned in (that number climbing to over 36 million during the next few months). Also, within 24 hours of the debut, www.disney-channel.com had scored 1.2 million hits with 500,000 people downloading the lyrics of the songs.

Executive producer Bill Borden was shocked by the response. "In every showing it's had," he says, "it's won its time slot, across the board, every time. It's beaten everything else on cable. It's set a record for the Disney Channel as being the highest-watched movie in its first showing, and the highest-watched movie in its second showing. The kids all love the movie. We had a magical time making it. We had fun every day. There was magic all around."

By February, after seven weeks in release, the soundtrack album was #1 on *Billboard*'s Top 200 Albums chart, with the disc quickly going multi-platinum. Also showcasing initial response to the songs from the film, "Breaking Free" jumped from #86 to #4 on the *Billboard* Pop 100 Singles Chart, a rise which took place over the course of just one week (making it the fastest-rising single ever!). A week later, it reached number one. In the course of that same month, *nine* singles from *HSM* were on the Hot 100 chart, five of which were in the Top 40.

Also impressive was the number of orders Disney Channel On Demand and Verizon's Video-On-Demand received. On Cablevision, orders for the film were 2,080% above the average number of Disney Channel On Demand orders, not including premieres.

Things continued from there. Reported Business Wire on March 16, "Sales of the platinum-selling *High School Musical* continue to rise with an 8% increase over last-week's sales. The 138,035 units scanned for the week of March 8 secured the #3 spot on the *Billboard* Top 200 chart. Digital sales also were a huge component of the soundtrack's success. This week alone 64,208 single tracks were sold digitally, and to date over 1 million single tracks have been purchased digitally, primarily through Apple Computer's iTunes Music Store."

The same report made mention of the fact that the soundtrack had generated a platinum single with "Breaking Free" and four gold singles represented by "What I've Been Looking For," "We're All in This Together," "Start of Something New" and "Get'cha Head in the Game." Additionally,

"It's set a record for the Disney Channel as being the highest-watched movie in its first showing, and the highest-watched movie in its second showing."

the album itself stood at number one on the *Billboard* Soundtrack chart, a position it had held for five out of the seven previous weeks, and the *Billboard* Kids chart, where it had been for eight consecutive weeks.

By April, a karaoke version was a hit, particularly among fans who were encouraged to hold parties and sing along to the film. Also, three music videos culled from the movie quickly joined the 12 most-popular video downloads at iTunes. Word then got out that a DVD release was being planned for May and that *High School Musical 2* was being put into motion, as well as a stage version and possibly a touring concert version. Reported the Associated Press, "Cell phone ring tones from the movie are going on sale. In June, Disney will export *High School Musical* to its cable channels in 23 other countries, including Taiwan, India, Japan, Australia, New Zealand, England, France, Spain and Germany."

On April 21, Disney announced that the 11th and 12th broadcasts of *High School Musical*, which were airing that night, would consist of a dance-along version, which provided a step-by-step choreography of the film's dances, and the previously aired sing-along karaoke version. Interestingly, it was also noted that the National Basketball Association had adopted the film's song "Get'cha Head in the Game" for use in a series of promo spots.

Scott Garner, Disney Channel's Senior V.P. of Programming, says, "We conceived the dance-along idea after we saw how successful the sing-along was. The movie keys into the popularity of singing and dancing. We've been able to respond to viewers. The dance-along idea actually came from kids writing to us wondering how they could learn the dance steps. One thing led to another, and it's just snowballed."

In early May, Wireless News reported that 500 Limited Too and 100 of its sister stores Justice would be exclusively carrying a line of tween merchandise inspired by the film which will, according to Disney, "combine the fun and spirited themes of the movie with catchy phrases from the original soundtrack and the likenesses of the movie's cast." Lisa Avent, V.P. of TV Licensing for Disney Consumer Products, said, "The response to *High School Musical* from teens and tweens has been phenomenal and has created great demand for a merchandise program that will allow them to bring the movie into their own environment. Limited Too will help us to reach this key demographic with a line that will extend the movie's inherent messages of optimism, self-expression and creativity." Future plans called for an expanded line of *HSM* apparel, accessories, home décor and stationery.

Newsweek reported that starting in June *High School Musical* would be going abroad, into about 100 countries with dubbed dialogue but songs remaining as they were in the original version. Noted Disney's Rich Ross, "This is our first orchestrated rollout overseas."

With all that was happening, Disney's Matt Palmer pointed out, "We have a huge hit on our hands. There's just an appetite for it. Whatever we do with this, kids are eating it up. We now have to figure out how to continue delivering this incredible film to kids in unique ways."

Hollywood Records followed up on the double-platinum success of the film's original soundtrack by a 2-disc "special edition" soundtrack on May 23. Disc number one features the original soundtrack plus the B5 hip-hop version of "Get'cha Head in the Game" as well as the accompanying music video, accessible through ROM drives. The special edition's second CD+Graphic (CD+G) disc provides karaoke versions for eight of the most popular songs, including "Breaking Free," "We're All in This Together" and "Start of Something New." The packaging also features complete song lyrics, a double-sided locker poster and, in a Walt Disney Records' first, a certificate for an exclusive, free "Get'cha Head in the Game" ringtone.

As if this wasn't enough for fans, at the same time a novelization of the film was published and the DVD edition was released. That DVD contains extras such as "Learning the Moves," in which Kenny Ortega, Ashley and Lucas attempt to teach viewers the

moves to "Bop to the Top"; a never-before-seen music video for "I Can't Take My Eyes Off of You," the music video of "We're All in This Together," and a behind-the-scenes look at the making of the film. Not surprisingly, the *HSM* phenomenon showed no signs of slowing down; on its first day of release the DVD sold 400,000 copies (with 1.2 million sold after six days).

Just before the DVD release, the cast was thrilled when Disney threw a red carpet premiere party at the El Capitan Theater in Hollywood. Following a screening of the film, they attended an after-party at the Hollywood

& Highland Center, the permanent home of the Oscars. There they were besieged by fans. Of all the attention, Zac offered at the time, "You know what? It's great. I'm so excited to have it. I just can't get caught up in it. Otherwise I won't stay focused. It's very awesome and it's so exciting."

Marvels Disney executive Gary Marsh, "They're great kids. They understand that this is a little bit of lightning in a bottle, and it's a moment in time for them to really shine. At the same time, I have to say that I'm not surprised by the success of the movie. What is surprising, though, is that what started out as a movie has become a movement. What's happened is kids are saying, 'How do we connect with this property?' They're the ones who after Christmas said, 'Oh my gosh, I can't find the CD in stores yet. Let me go to iTunes and buy it.' So what's really gratifying for us, as a company that's often accused of over marketing, is this really rose up as a grassroots enterprise."

Admits Disney's Rich Ross, "I wasn't surprised that people loved it. I have to say I'm surprised it's the number one album of the year. That it's the fastest-selling TV movie on DVD product ever. These are the things you sit there and say, 'Well, I can dream.' And then the dream becomes a reality. I knew we had something wonderful that everyone loved. I didn't realize when I said the word 'everyone' I meant *everyone*. I think it probably sums up everything we do. It sums up sort of the ethos of the channel. We've been developing talent for a long time. We had an incredible cast. We've been supporting musical works. So I think there were a lot of antecedents that we've been working on, and then kismet gives it a moment."

"I don't think anyone would have predicted, even in our wildest dreams, what a stunning success it would become," adds ABC-Disney TV Group President Ann Sweeney. "We've made a lot of tremendous movies. There has been, to my mind, a lot of wonderful, wonderful movies. But you never really know what is going to be that movie, that television show that just absolutely grabs people and doesn't let them go. And that's what *High School Musical* became. It was just the perfect alignment of the stars."

On May 25 the *Richmond Times Dispatch* reported, "Radio Disney will hold a *High School Musical* Talent Competition... Children 14 and younger can sing along to select tracks from the soundtrack to win prizes and qualify for the chance to travel to Los Angeles and record a song that will be featured on Radio Disney."

On June 19, Mattel, Inc. announced that they would be introducing a new DVD board game based on *HSM*, which will allow players to enter their favorite moments from the film and interact with the DVD to complete challenges and move through the East High campus in an effort to make final callback auditions. Tim Kilpin, General Manager and Senior V.P. of Mattel, enthuses, "We are excited to bring this smash-hit movie to life in a way that lets kids immerse themselves in an interactive game and be a part of the *High School Musical* phenomenon. The game integrates audition elements such as memorable video clips, songs and dances from the show that kids will enjoy and love.

The game is a perfect addition to Mattel's growing portfolio of interactive games."

In July, The Talent Co. announced that it had acquired the first New York–area stage rights to *High School Musical*. Auditions began in September with rehearsals starting in early November. At about the same time, it was announced that the film had been nominated for six Emmys in the categories of Outstanding Children's Program; Best

Choreography; Outstanding Casting for a Miniseries, Movie or Special; Outstanding Directing for a Miniseries, Movie or a Special; and two for Outstanding Music and Lyrics.

Malaysian singer Vince Chong and Singapore's Alicia Pan were brought aboard to record an Asian version of "Breaking Free" to tie in to a broadcast of *High School Musical*. Says Ashok Miranda, Creative Director for Walt Disney Television International, "We were looking for new faces in the region who are making their mark in the music industry." Adds Vince, "I felt good singing a song about believing in yourself, moving out of your comfort zone, breaking out of your shell and going after your dreams."

The film's success definitely continued overseas. The soundtrack went gold in New Zealand and when it aired in Australia, *HSM* was the second highest-rated film on the country's airwaves. Both accomplishments were no doubt aided by the fact Zac, Vanessa, Ashley and Monique made the international promo rounds.

To support the debut of *High School Musical* in England, Disney Channel UK came up with a school-based promotional campaign. They created a CD-ROM aimed at students aged 9 to 13, and sent it to 12,000 schools to encourage children to express themselves through song and dance.

At the 2006 Teen Choice Awards, *High School Musical* took home Surfboards for: Choice Comedy/Musical, Choice Chemistry (Zac Efron/Vanessa Anne Hudgens) and Breakout Star (Zac Efron). And then at the 58th Annual Primetime Emmy Awards, the film won for Choreo-graphy and Children's Program and the entire cast was on hand to accept.

The influence of *High School Musical* continued to be felt around the world throughout the rest of the year, with the stage version premiering at New York's Stagedoor Manor in August, and numerous others in development for around the country. And while the cast of the film was together for the film's UK premiere, much of the final quarter of 2006 was spent with them involved with their own projects: Zac in Toronto shooting the new movie version of the Broadway musical *Hairspray*, which itself was based on the 1988 non-musical film of the same name; Vanessa recording, releasing and promoting her debut album, *V*; Corbin recording his solo album while shooting the Disney film *Jump In!*; Ashley working hard on the new season of *The Suite Life of Zack & Cody* while simultaneously recording her first album for Warner Bros. Records; Monique participating in ABC's hit series *Dancing with the Stars*; and Lucas shooting the latest *Halloweentown* TV movie. Everyone seemed to go off in their own directions, but fans can take solace in the fact that they'd come back together again in 2007 to shoot the first of two planned *High School Musical* sequels.

LESSONS LEARNED

The question that surrounds the entire pop culture phenomenon known as *High School Musical* is just why has it connected with the audience in the way that it has? Disney's Gary Marsh offers this possibility: "The reality is that a kid's world is incredibly tense and full of pressure and anguish. If what we can do is provide the release valve, provide the jubilation, the celebration that is what kids are looking for, if we do it right. It may be corny, but it sure feels good."

Many believe the audience connects with the film's underlying message: giving in to peer pressure can be a mistake and it's more important to be true to yourself than live up to the ideals of others.

"Walk your own path," Zac declares. "Don't listen to all the pressures that come from the outside world. Troy starts out as this hotshot stud, but he's been given that name by his peers — it's not really who he is. By the end of the movie, he discovers that he can be himself and have just as much fun. He goes through this great transformation. By the end of the movie, he's even cooler."

"It's a great message," enthuses Ashley. "And when I was in high school, I kind of went through the same thing. There are all these cliques and it's really important, because everyone can relate. I mean,

95

even older adults can relate because you know those characters so well in our movie. And it's like stepping out of that clique and feeling like you can say what you are, what else you want to do and not find yourself as a person after school, but do it *in* school. I think it's important for kids to learn that. After you come out of school, you realize that you just don't have to be the basketball player or the volleyball player. You can actually do something else. But in high school, you're so intimidated by the people you're around and the cliques that say you have to stay that way. But this movie kind of breaks that down and says while you're in school, you can actually do this and you can be a cook and a basketball player and not feel that you're dorky or anything."

Both Monique's and Corbin's favorite scenes in the film are very similar in the sense that their characters are going through arcs that parallel each other and, in turn, reinforce the themes of the film.

"Being the antagonist along with Corbin," Monique begins, "my favorite scene is the one where I was trying to convince Vanessa's character of Gabriella as to why she should not attempt to audition for this musical. I'm expressing to her that we are a different breed of people; that you have the 'brainies' and you have the jocks and they're very separate. I don't agree with that in real life, obviously, but I love that just in terms of my character arc to go from having a strong feeling and then seeing how it affected the characters and seeing how things really started to fall apart, even though we were trying to make things better, so definitely the

scene where I was coaching her to stay on our team."

Corbin notes, "Mine intertwines with the same scene; it bounces back and forth between me actually trying to convince [Troy] to say he doesn't want to do [the musical] anymore. I'm actually filming him secretly. At the same time, Taylor is in the room with Gabriella, showing her that videotape of him saying he doesn't want to do it anymore. From a character standpoint, to be able to put that different side of it was interesting. Throughout the movie my character is a very outgoing guy. I mean, he's very happy, very energetic and this is the one moment where you see this mischievous side to him. It's something that you play, those two sides of the character."

In terms of the story, Monique believes these scenes are extremely valuable for kids because they deal with peer pressure. "It's actually a little bit of an exaggeration of a situation of someone going through that and making so much of an elaborate effort to convince you of something," she explains. "But I do think that peer pressure is a huge thing in high school and middle school. It even exists with adults. It's something that's definitely plaguing us, so I think it's really cool for kids to be able to see that, to experience that and relate to such a feeling. I think it does feel overwhelming sometimes if someone is shoving an idea down your throat.

"Even with myself growing up," Monique continues, "I was told that I was good at English and things like that, so that's what I focused on. Of course, I had a natural inclination to perform and do theater and

"It was music that brought the whole school together and made us accomplish what we wanted."

stuff, but what if someone would have told me that I could have done something else or what if someone would have tutored me in science or math? Maybe I would have been able to excel in those areas as well. I love that we got to be part of that story."

In Vanessa's opinion, another message of the film is the notion of conquering your fears. "Gabriella and Troy start off as the genius girl and the hot jock," she says. "It was music that brought the whole school together and made us accomplish what we wanted."

Returning to the question of why so popular, not *everyone* is surprised by the film's success. "It starts with the words on the page, and if people connect with that, you can't go wrong," Kenny Ortega opines. "You begin with something that is accessible and strong and you put that team around you. It doesn't happen all the time. You can have 14 years between those kinds of projects. It's the experience that you look forward to. Each time you hope that's what it's going to be like."

Considering this, Zac points out, "It's a story that has been told so many times. The only thing different about it is the music. We threw in three minutes of music between all the drama and comedy — I think that has to be what got kids' attention. It makes the movie a lot more fun. It's much more interesting when you can become a part of it through the music. This kind of film is something that we're really missing these days. I grew up with it, watching *Grease* and the musical Disney animated movies. Music was a part of films. That's what made me excited. I think we brought that back a little bit, and it's so different to be on the other side of these movies. You watch *Grease* and it's so magical — cars fly away and people are flying in a song, and everyone knows the dance to the same song. And it doesn't matter if it makes sense, because you are so into the movie at that point. You're just watching it and having the warmest feeling. You don't want it to end. To be able to hopefully provide that feeling to other people is just amazing. I want people to watch it and to feel sad when it's ending."

Vanessa explains that growing up doing musical theater and hearing that the Disney Channel was doing a musical instantly triggered a spark of interest on her part. "The fact that it hasn't been done in so long, it had to have some kind of impact on kids," she says. "Musicals are a great thing because they integrate singing and dance scenes. To start off with that, I knew it was something that was going to be really good and big, and knowing Kenny was going to be a part of it, I thought it couldn't go wrong. But no one knew it was going to be this big. It has become a phenomenon. It's hysterical, especially when I go out with my friends and people start doing the scenes for us. It's just funny."

Gary Marsh came to realize how strong an impact the film was having when everyone around the office began asking for copies of the soundtrack prior to *HSM* airing. "They wanted to play it in their cars and take it home for their kids," he recollects. "But to have ever dreamed this could go to number one on the *Billboard* chart *twice* no less, that was beyond my wildest dreams. And I can dream pretty big."

CAN'T TAKE OUR EYES OFF OF THEM

On a more personal level as far as the cast is concerned, there is no doubt the popularity of the film placed them directly in the media spotlight, increasing their fame dramatically.

For Zac, what's been most exciting is experiencing people's response to the film. "Watching kids react to the film is incredible," he smiles. "Adults are able to hide their true feelings. When they see you they may dumb down or they have not even seen the movie in the first place. With kids you get a very pure sense of joy when they see you, which is really fun. I remember from when I was a kid. You used to see the people you look up to and when they signed that little piece of paper, it made your day. I think we had the ability to do that."

The cast got a true sense of the film's impact on people when they attended a YMCA-like school. "It was a Saturday," says Zac, "and all the kids were actually putting on a performance of the show. We went in and read lines with them. They were so serious about it. They were having so much fun doing the scene as us. It was just an incredible experience. We got up and read lines."

Vanessa adds, "It was very rewarding to know they liked it."

"We actually had a boy come over to us," notes Ashley, "and he explained that he was a basketball jock but that after watching our movie, he got up the courage to go out for a musical in the school. He got the lead for *Peter Pan*."

For Ashley, the success of the film more or less doubled the number of people who approach her — which says a lot, considering the popularity of her Disney Channel series, *The Suite Life of Zack & Cody*. Obviously there could be a downside to such attention, which she's very aware of. "But I know when strangers are lurking in my neighborhood," she emphasizes. "I know all the kids on my street, because I used to babysit them. Now teenagers are camping out on my street waiting for me to come out of my house. Recently four teenagers followed me to the end of my road and my dad's, like, 'Oh, no, here we go.'"

When he appeared on *Jimmy Kimmel*, Zac related one story that demonstrated how things were changing for him. The host had asked him if he had grown women throwing themselves at him, to which Zac responded, "It's funny you should mention that. I was buying a CD the other day and I looked up and there was a rather large girl — she looked to be 13 or 14 and she was 5'10" or a little taller — and she actually sort of

"I've come to see myself as a chameleon, because I almost blend in with other people, so I don't usually get recognized."

tackled me and kissed me on the lips. *That was an experience."* Additionally, while appearing on MTV's *Total Request Live,* he related this story: "The movie had just been released and I went to Tower Records in Sherman Oaks, and there was an unrelated autograph-signing and tons of kids. I walked in and the whole room went silent. I sort of looked around, everyone was pointing and I had to sort of back out and run back to my car. It was pretty crazy."

Vanessa points out that she seems to avoid the crowds for the most part. "I've come to see myself as a chameleon, because I almost blend in with other people, so I don't usually get recognized. Every now and then, if I'm wearing my hair back or something, then I do. I think it's fun. How many kids get recognized?"

She finds the experience uplifting because the kids she meets and the e-mails she receives often credit her for being a role model. "It's just a great personal accomplishment," Vanessa says earnestly, "and being recognized isn't going to last forever, so I may as well enjoy it as long as I can."

The only time it does become a problem, she points out, is when she's out with celebrity friends and they're just trying to spend some time with each other and hang out, but at the same time she recognizes that that's something that goes with the territory of being a celebrity. One particular example comes to mind: she and Zac had gone out to the movies, somehow putting out of their minds the little fact they were now stars on the Disney Channel and it was increasingly more likely that they would be recognized

in public. They went to a fairly popular movie theater and started to notice some girls hovering around them. When the film ended, things intensified a bit.

"We had to walk out with everybody and there were tons and tons and tons of kids waiting in the lobby," she laughs. "We ended up taking pictures and all. It's kind of crazy and an adrenaline rush, but it's fun."

Ashley adds, "Fans are surprised to see the whole cast hanging together at the mall. Normally, you wouldn't see the whole cast of *Ocean's 11* out at the mall."

Monique admits that she's a little amazed at all that has been happening. "The energy we had between each other was rare and special," she explains, "and I knew we were in good hands with Kenny Ortega, but I had no idea we would some day be on the *Today Show* and *Good Morning America* — big shows that are staples of American culture — and that *HSM* would become a pop culture phenomenon. It is so exciting that it has taken on a life of its own."

Ashley drives home the point that all of this success and everything they've been through has not been the result of an overnight sensation, as the media has often suggested. "It just kind of progressed in every way," she says. "It was like a surprise every day. You would wake up and it was like getting a new present each day. It was just so cool and it's so much fun that kids are enjoying something that we loved making. It just had so much going for it: great story, great producers, great director, great cast that got along, great music — all of which really made it so huge."

The impact of the film certainly wasn't lost on executive producer Bill Borden, who shared a particular anecdote about adults rather than kids: "I was playing tennis with three other 50-year-old men like myself. We are all very well-placed in the movie industry and the other three guys had no idea that I did *High School Musical*. And one of the very big shot lawyers on the other side said he happened to catch it for the 15th time or something in his house and saw my name by accident. He wanted to know if I was the same person that he'd been playing with for

For Corbin, interactions with fans have been rewarding to a large degree. He reflects that one kid came up to him to let him know that he was a dancer too, that he was a fan and hoped that one day the two of them might be able to work together. "I thought that was awesome," says Corbin. "I was so honored he felt that way."

the last three years. I said, 'Yes, it's me.' The game stopped as the three guys wanted to discuss the movie. All three of them had seen it, I think, 20 or 30 times among them. They had seen it because of their kids and they wanted to discuss it."

Despite popular belief, no one involved really expected *High School Musical* to have the kind of instant impact that it would ultimately have.

"Honestly," says Zac, "I don't think any of us had that high kind of expectations. Disney Channel movies are great for a select audience. I think that it was just luck. I think all of us came together and when we sort of clicked on set, that was when I started to realize that this thing could be big. We all got along so great — the producers, the director and we all came together. I think our connection on set just really made the movie what it is."

Ashley adds, "I agree that a lot of it has to do with our chemistry. Plus Disney was really supportive. We have great producers, a great writer. It is the *Grease* for this generation. Kids don't have that. The music and all the elements put together just caught on. The characters may be over-dramatized a little bit, but everyone has been to school and you know exactly the types of characters we're dealing with."

Opines Lucas, "None of us expected this success, even though

"None of us expected this success, even though we had an amazing time on set. It was one of those life experiences you will remember for a really long time."

we had an amazing time on set. It was one of those life experiences you will remember for a really long time. But that was all I expected to take away from it. I just thought it would be a wonderful experience for the memory bank. But then it came out and blew up — it mutated into something spectacular. It took me a while — probably a month — to recognize and acknowledge the fact it was so successful, and it is very cool, I must say."

During production — and in retrospect, given the audience's response to it — many of the people involved with the film wondered why *High School Musical* wasn't being released theatrically rather than aired on the Disney Channel. In the end, though, almost everyone recognized that broadcasting *HSM* on television was the best way to go.

Lucas points out that "this was definitely edited for television and for children. I think that there's a reason it hasn't hit theaters. Not because of a lack of integrity or quality, but simply for the fact of how it's formulated. It's very quick and fast-moving. It just has the ebbs and flows of something where you know when a commercial break is going to come in. I think with a little extra time and some more editing and stuff, it might have been suitable for that. But for what it is, I think it's perfect for the Disney Channel."

"The Disney Channel goes directly to the audience that we would want to see the movie," Zac muses. "So it's like we can bypass all the people that would go see the movie [in theaters] and call it cheesy or would hold it to a different standard. I think having it on the channel allowed kids to see

it immediately; they didn't have to get driven to the movie theater to see it. I also think that the Disney Channel does a good job of picking good kids, and I think maybe other places let a few slip by. I think in our movie in particular, they picked a dang good cast. I give everyone in that movie credit, and we didn't make it too over-the-top, which could have been a downfall. We made it more realistic, and I think it reached a larger audience and more people could relate to it because of that."

Monique offers, "It would have been cool for me to see the dance numbers on the big screen. Every time we've seen clips and things when we're in a different venue, it's really phenomenal. I do have a passion for big dance numbers, like the cafeteria scene in *Fame* and so on. I would have loved to have seen 'We're All In This Together' coming at you. I think that would have been really cool."

"It was funny," Corbin offers, "because during the actual shooting, you're sitting there going, 'Why isn't this a feature movie?' It was really kind of the feeling that it could be. It's not until after you see the final product that you go, 'Okay, I get the reason why.' It's just the way it was filmed. But as Monique said, I would have loved to have seen that."

Disney's Michael Healy explains, "We like it kid-driven, but open to adults. As Bill said, I think a lot of adults have gotten a chance to see this and enjoy it. But the way in is their children; the people we're really serving are those children. Who knows what it would have done at the box office?"

BREAKING FREE
The Stars Go Solo

There has become a tradition at Disney — whether it be through the feature film or television departments — to take popular young stars and do their corporate best to turn them into music artists. Sometimes the results have been very good, as in the case of Hilary Duff who started out as the star of the Disney Channel's *Lizzie McGuire*, eventually became a pop star with millions of album sales behind her. Other times, the results have been less positive, such as the effort to do the same with *Freaky Friday* and *Herbie: Fully Loaded* star Lindsay Lohan. In a sense, the process is akin to capturing lightning in a bottle. Difficult to do, for sure, but if successful, the results can be pure magic.

With *High School Musical*, there's no doubt the studio wanted to turn to the talented cast that helped transform the film into a sensation and see if they could sustain solo careers via a contract with Disney's Hollywood Records. On a corporate level — and from a financial point of view — this idea must have seemed like going after the individual members of the Beatles (if you don't know, ask your parents!) with recording contracts. Why settle for a single Beatles album when you could get four individual albums from John Lennon, Paul McCartney, George Harrison and Ringo Starr? The question, of course, was whether or not Zac, Vanessa, Ashley, Corbin, Lucas and Monique would be interested in signing with Hollywood Records.

"At this point," says Zac, "if I make an album, people can get confused. I am an actor who can just do a little bit of singing. A lot of the kids in *HSM* have a lot of different values and aspirations. I am just here to act and be in that category." Speaking of Zac's singing, there was a bit of controversy that arose when one of the film's composers, Andrew Seeley, went public saying he sang Zac's part, but then it was stated that the final film features a blending of their voices.

For his part, Lucas feels similarly, noting that he's been playing music since the eighth grade and singing for just as long. For him, it's always been an artistic release, so for the time being an actual recording contract *doesn't* interest him. "I want to establish myself in acting first," he explains, "before getting into a side project of music. If I were to take a side project now, I would feel I am not focusing on what I came out here to do. I don't want to spread myself too thin. I want to be established as an actor and then someday take a two-month break and put all my efforts into a record."

Monique can be added to that camp too, as she emphasizes that she started out, first and foremost, as a dancer/actress and that singing more or less entered the equation at a later date. Nonetheless, "I would definitely take a recording contract if someone offered one, but that is not what I set out to do when I became an actress."

With three of the *HSM* cast members expressing little interest in a recording career, Disney was still hopeful that the remaining three cast members would sign with Hollywood Records. But one of the *HSM* six-pack — Ashley Tisdale — ultimately elected to sign with Warner Bros. Records.

"I wanted to be taken seriously as a true artist," she says, "but the fans haven't seen that side of me because I've been playing characters as well as singing. That's really why my motive was to go to Warner Bros. Records, because that would give me a chance to prove I'm not just a Disney star who thought it would be a great marketing tool to sing and put out an album for fun. It's something that I take seriously and I want to support fully.

"I felt if I had gone to Hollywood Records," Ashley elaborates, "people would have taken me as the girl who was on Disney and trying to be the Hilary Duff kind of

"At this point, if I make an album, people can get confused. I am an actor who can just do a little bit of singing."

thing, and that's not what I'm trying to say at all. I'm saying that I grew up in theater, I grew up with music, I do write some music and this is something I'm taking seriously. With every label I went to, I said, 'This is not something I want to ride off the success of *High School Musical* with. This is a project I've wanted to do forever, and now have people asking for me. I don't want the label to just kind of put it out there because of the phenomenon of *High School Musical*. I want this to be completely separate from my acting career.' And Warner Bros. Records totally respected that." Ashley's debut album would reach stores in February 2007.

The first solo artist from *High School Musical* who *did* sign with Hollywood Records — and whose debut, *V*, hit stores on September 26, 2006 — was Vanessa Anne Hudgens.

Amazingly, Vanessa signed with Hollywood and recorded the album less than two months later. While her original concept was to create a dance album, she instead decided to go with a variety of genres. "The songs were already there," she says of the tracks written for her, "so I just went with the flow. Most albums have a genre and stick to it, but I decided to have some fun with the whole pop idea. There's some pop-rock, some R&B-pop, some electric-dance-pop. I just had fun with it and did my own thing." And in terms of coming up with the title, Vanessa points out, "My manager just said, *V*. I put a peace sign up and thought, 'That's perfect.' I have so many ideas for merchandise, like jeans, with Vs on them. Corbin calls me 'V,' and it's my favorite nickname."

"Most albums have a genre and stick to it, but I decided to have some fun with the whole pop idea."

The Cheetah Girls: Kiely Williams, Sabrina Bryan and Adrienne Bailon

Her first single was "Come Back to Me," which deals with relationships and the one guy that got away, while the song "Whatever Will Be" is all about letting go of the past and embracing the present. "It's the definition of me, because that's my motto," she explains.

"Say OK" deals with the notion of peer pressure — a theme she's very familiar with thanks to *High School Musical* — and particularly from a guy whose intentions don't seem to be all that honorable. The song "Afraid" had Vanessa torn between letting herself fall in love and pushing away the boy she likes, scared of feeling the same heartache from her past. "Promise" reminds the listener that it's okay to be yourself and if someone doesn't like it, it's too bad for them. Again, a perfect theme for people who had fallen in love with *High School Musical*.

Vanessa has no problem admitting that for her debut she didn't write any of the songs, depending, instead, on the expertise of others. "I figured my first album I'll leave it to the professionals," she says. "Once I know the process, I'll get my creative juices flowing."

Helping to ensure that Vanessa connected with her fans — and would indeed have the opportunity to record a second album — Disney arranged things so that she could serve as one of the opening acts for the Cheetah Girls tour. Similar to the situation with *HSM*, the Cheetah Girls began life as a Disney Channel TV movie; it was so successful that it resulted in real-life music careers for its stars.

Which leaves Corbin Bleu — what decision did he make? When looking for a label for himself, he ultimately chose to stay within the Disney fold. In fact, he began working on the album for Hollywood Records shortly after returning from Toronto where he shot the Disney Channel TV movie *Jump In!*.

Of this March 2007 album, Corbin explains, "It's sort of a pop and R&B feel. I also play piano, so think a male Alicia Keys or Usher or John Legend, or, on the pop side, kind of Justin Timberlake. That's what I'm shooting for."

So in the end, only 50 percent of *High School Musical*'s primary cast decided that the timing was right for them to pursue their solo music careers. Thankfully the inescapable fact was that when it comes to music, they would be reunited for the soundtrack of *High School Musical 2*.

HSM HITS THE STAGE

During the summer of 2006, the team behind *High School Musical* announced the movie was ready for its next incarnation as a stage show. In the end, it will no doubt turn out to be just as significant as the film itself in that it will reach students around the country, be staged at both Disneyland and Disney World and hit professional arenas as well.

In a joint announcement Disney Theatrical Productions and Music Theater International (MTI) confirmed that the first production of *HSM* as a live musical would take place at Stagedoor Manor, the renowned kids/teen theater summer camp based in Sheldrake, New York. At the same time, it was announced that amateur productions would be mounted at Green Valley High School in Henderson, Nevada; James H. Blake High School in Silver Springs, Maryland; Woodhills High School in Pittsburgh, Pennsylvania; Upper Dublin High School in Fort Washington, Pennsylvania; Woodlands High School in The Woodlands, Texas; Steven F.

"It is simply astounding to think of how many young artists will have the opportunity to work on *High School Musical*."

Andrea Ross (Gabriella), Dylan Tedaldi (Ryan), Olivia Baackes (Sharpay) and Jordan Campbell (Troy)

Austin High School in Austin, Texas; and New Albany High School in New Albany, Indiana. Additionally, the first professional production was announced for January 13–21, 2007, at Atlanta's Theater of the Stars.

"We have already received an overwhelming response from schools all over the country," Thomas Schumacher, producer at Disney Theatrical Productions, says. "With Disney titles, including *Beauty and the Beast* and *Aida*, already having been performed in over 1,500 schools, by the end of 2007 we can anticipate some 2,000 schools will produce *High School Musical*. That would mean, at the end of the first year alone over 60,000 students will have the thrill of bringing live theater to their communities. It is simply astounding to think of how many young artists will have the opportunity to work on *High School Musical*. As someone who grew up working in amateur productions and dreaming of a career in the theater, *High School Musical* will give these students their first taste of presenting a show."

Stagedoor Manor was founded by Carl and Elsie Samuelson in 1976 in partnership with creative director Jack Romano and it is owned and produced by his daughters Cindy and Debra Samuelson. Deciding to move past shows for the very young, they turned to more challenging and edgy material. As a result, the camp has a history of staging everything from Sondheim to Brecht to Shakespeare. Committed to talent and experience on all levels, there is no audition for campers to attend. Stagedoor simply

"I think *High School Musical* was created with the intention of speaking to every teen. We have *all* slammed a locker with these characters and identify with the crush of the social structure."

looks for kids who love theater. Over the course of a summer, 40 shows are produced in seven on-site spaces, and when not in rehearsals, classes are offered in every level of performing arts. Agents, managers and casting directors discovered long ago that Stagedoor was the place to find future stars. (Celebrity alumni include Natalie Portman, Mandy Moore and Zach Braff.) At the same time, kids discover a world of friends and family who understand their passion and commitment. For an inside look at Stagedoor, check out the film *Camp*, written and produced by former camper Todd Graff.

In detailing how *HSM* ended up at Stagedoor Manor, camp production director Konnie Kittrell explains, "When Music Theater International announced plans for the project, I requested that Stagedoor be considered. We had worked with MTI and Disney the summer before on a Broadway Jr. workshop production of *Aida*. During the first session of 2006, Marty Johnson [head of the education department at MTI] was staging a reading of *Rent* with us and I asked him every day about the possibilities of *High School Musical* for third session. I felt we were the perfect venue for their first run. Our kids can mount anything in three weeks, and the companies would be able to

"We wanted Darbus [the drama teacher] to be 'out there,' eccentric, but someone who makes every kid in her program want to give his or her best, who is the hero to her students, a real mentor."

tweak as we went. We didn't get the go-ahead until the week before auditions."

Stagedoor director Larry Nye, who has been involved with the camp for 10 of its summer sessions, points out that there was a great deal of debate over whether *HSM* should be approached as a Broadway musical or a national tour, before the decision was made to go directly to schools. "There is money to be made," he says, "but I know that Konnie Kittrell worked hard to bring this product to Stagedoor. Disney needed a company ASAP and we were available. We had worked with them and MTI in the past with positive results."

One point Kittrell makes is that neither Stagedoor nor Disney had any idea of the sheer volume of work that still needed to be done before the curtain could go up on *High School Musical*. "Pages of script came in by fax," says Kittrell. "There was no official score to teach the music. Bryan

Louiselle and David Simpatico [music supervisor and writer of the show's "book" or script] were working til all hours to meet our deadlines. They were fabulous! E-mails flew back and forth with ideas and suggestions. Technical questions, character questions, costume questions! We were a week into production before we all agreed to use music on track instead of the usual piano accompany. Our kids had never worked with tracks before and had about two days to figure it out. Also a challenge for the scenic people — *High School Musical* takes place in a lot of locations and the climax of the show takes place in three places at once."

They were concerned with keeping the values and elements of the original, but Disney assured them they wanted every group to take the show and make it their own. The kids were familiar with the film, but very excited about adding their own energy to the project. The trick, of course, was finding the right kids for the roles.

"I think *High School Musical* was created with the intention of speaking to every teen," says Kittrell. "We have *all* slammed a locker with these characters and identify with the crush of the social structure. I admit, as far as looks go, we followed the movie. Finding the perfect look combined with the necessary talent was a challenge. Ryan and Sharpay had to dance as well as sing. Troy and Gabriella must have solid rock voices. And basketball? Ha! Not many theater kids play sports. *High School Musical* is about a sports star who learns he can sing. We needed a singer who could learn to play basketball in two weeks. In fact, only one Wildcat had basketball experience. Fortunately Larry Nye, our director/choreographer, had been the son of a high school basketball coach himself. He turned the whole game into choreography."

In terms of adapting *High School Musical* from a TV movie to the stage, writer

David Simpatico explains that about two years ago Disney asked him to adapt the animated film *Alice in Wonderland* for the stage. "That's when I met Bryan Louiselle," he explains. "We instantly clicked; our sense of humor ran the gamut from *Gilligan's Island* to Gilbert and Sullivan. We had a ball updating and adapting the *Alice* film and Disney was very happy with what we turned out. Then, in January 2006, I got a call from them asking if I would be interested in adapting this movie musical that just had its first viewing on the Disney Channel, *High School Musical*. I had seen it already because I'm a sucker for musicals about musicals, and said, 'Sure,' as long as I could be teamed up with Bryan."

Louiselle adds, "David and I share an odd sense of humor. That worked in our favor plus the fact that we work really quickly led, I think, to our being asked to adapt *High School Musical*. Disney folks —

particularly our executive producer, Steve Fickinger — knew that the timetable was, um, brisk, not to put too fine a point on it."

The first thing they had to deal with was zeroing in on what "70 billion kids" knew and loved about *HSM* and staying true to that. "If you know any 9- to 13-year-olds, they've all memorized this thing — every line, every note, every vocal nuance, and there was a lot of pressure to give 'em what they know, what they want," Louiselle details. "There was also a need to make the songs more theatrical. The songs are treated in the film almost as music videos. I don't mean that in a bad way — it's a movie, after all. But we had to finesse the storytelling aspects of the songs. In other words, to use the songs to carry the story forward and reveal character, not stop the momentum."

Simpatico agrees, adding that part of their problem was connected to one of the film's blessings: it was *so* popular. "No one expected it to turn into such a runaway hit, and no one ever expected it to turn into a cult hit to the point where kids around the world know every line and dance move. So we had to keep the spirit and story the kids knew, but had to open it up for the stage. Close-ups and short little scenes are made for film, but on stage we found we had to combine scenes, write completely new scenes and get rid of a bunch that didn't seem to work on stage. The stage is a medium focused on the word; film is focused on the eye, what we see. So we had to transmute a lot of the stuff in the film that was communicated visually to what could be done in real life, in front of an audience."

When approaching the adaptation, there were definitely elements of the film that both men wanted to retain, and certain changes they felt absolutely had to be made for the show to be successful with audiences.

"Nothing I say here in any way is meant to disparage anything in the movie," Louiselle emphasizes. "Seventy billion kids can't be wrong and there are a lot of wonderful messages in the movie: be yourself, follow your dream. Can't get more classically Disney than that. Theater as a valued means of self-expression. Love *that*. The *Romeo and Juliet* aspect with the jocks and the brainiacs as Montagues and Capulets. And a lot of the song hooks are just plain catchy. Didn't want to mess with that at *all*. But in terms of different directions —

David and I felt that theater, the idea of theater, was a little mocked in the movie. And that there was a missed opportunity to parallel kids with different interests — sports, academics, theater — to show how hard they all work at something they really love. We wanted Darbus [the drama teacher] to be 'out there,' eccentric, but someone who makes every kid in her program want to give his or her best, who is the hero to her students, a real mentor.

"Also, with a little more time to develop characters," he continues, "we wanted to give Sharpay and Ryan some humanity, to show why they are like they are. And David has done a wonderful job tracing everyone's journey. You can follow everyone from start to finish — not just the major players, but Kelsi, Chad, Taylor, Martha, Coach Bolton — and everyone gets to learn a little something, to be something at the end of the play that they weren't at the beginning."

Simpatico notes that the basic thrust of the story is that we are all free to be whatever we want to be. "I think that's the main reason the film has such appeal, because it reinforces the hope in kids that the universe is waiting for them to grow into whatever they may want to become. In the movie, the hopes and dreams are focused primarily on Gabby and Troy, but in the play, we wanted to open that up to include all the kids in the story, so that each of the main characters has something they are hoping for, yearning

for; some change they are trying to achieve. 'Start of Something New' is now a group number, culminating in the combined hopes of the student body facing a brand new year.

"I kept about 30 percent of the dialogue and reinvented a large part of it, opening it up on stage and exploring other characters, like Sharpay and Ryan, Zeke and Kelsi," he adds. "The main thing we changed, as Bryan said, was Ms. Darbus. When we sat around the table to discuss the rewrites of the play, we all agreed that the drama teachers in our past saved our lives, gave us the outlet that allowed us to pursue our dreams, so I wanted to reinvent that character along more solid lines. She is still kind of nutty, but

hopefully she comes across as someone who genuinely tries to help her students achieve their best, and who helps them do so. She has real impact now on Troy, helping him to tap into something new."

Musically, there are some notable differences between *High School Musical* the film and *High School Musical* the stage play. For starters, Louiselle wrote two new songs and expanded the theatrical context of some of the others, all of which has involved the ensemble a lot more than it originally was.

"'Start of Something New,' the song that Gabriella and Troy sing in the karaoke party, is now a big production number," he says. "The number starts as a device for Troy and Gabriella to meet, but then we return to

the first day of the semester, and now it's the start of something new for everyone. 'Bop to the Top,' which is Sharpay and Ryan's callback, is now also used in Act One to frame the auditions, à la 'God, I Hope I Get It' from *A Chorus Line.* And I changed the instrumentation from a synth-based, sometimes looped, sometimes dance-groove thing, which worked well in the movie, to a more straight ahead live-rock sound. Part of this was practical — Disney is licensing *HSM* with the orchestration, so it needs to be playable. But more important, I feel the rock grooves work better in the theater, are more immediate and more driving.

"Overall, I think — and pray — we did a pretty good job balancing familiarity with innovation," Louiselle smiles. "I hope, in other words, that the tweenies aren't going to hunt us down for meddling too much."

Simpatico points out that in the change of media, the relationship that probably changed the most was the one between Sharpay and Ryan. "I felt that Ryan had been very underused and was merely Sharpay's sidekick," he says, "but I wondered how the character would feel just being a sidekick, even though he had all this talent. So I added some scenes between him and his sister, exploring their dynamic and, at the end, it is Ryan who emerges as a kind of hero, growing into his own stature and helping his sister in the process. Also, I wanted to adjust the relationship between Troy and his dad to be overtly adversarial: they never call each other dad or son until the very end of the show; instead, they call each other Coach or Bolton. I wanted to show how the determination and narrow vision of the father would open up as he sees his son changing. Everyone changes for the good in the stage version. I hope so, anyway!"

For director Larry Nye, the biggest challenge for him was the staging of the "Bop to the Top" number toward the end of the show. "There was the basketball game, the science decathlon and the callbacks happening all at the same time," he says. "If I may say, I thought I did an amazing job making it work for the stage.

"I tried to pay homage to the movie," he continues. "It was very popular and a lot of the kids knew the dances. I took the essence of what I thought Mr. Ortega was trying to create with each scene and developed them in my own style. I have degrees in dance and a background as a choreographer, so I believe that movement is essential to musicals. Some of the choreography came to me on the spot. Some I worked after viewing the movie. Some I stole from other dances I had choreographed. I was so pleased with how I utilized Mr. Ortega's work without copying it. I did use the choreography for 'We're All in This Together,' because it was good and very popular with the kids. We had two weeks. I got a copy of the script one week before casting."

Speaking of the cast, Nye notes that the teens chosen from among the Stagedoor campers were very excited and worked extremely hard in the first week, suffered a bit from second-week burnout but rallied strongly in the end.

"I had to teach the jocks how to play basketball and then dance like basketball players," laughs Nye. "I played basketball and my father was a coach. As a young child, I would go to my father's games and hang out with the cheerleaders and then watch the game. My two sisters were cheerleaders, so I had a lot of exposure to cheering. I also coached the girls in the neighborhood before they tried out for the squad. I was always into movement. My lead's mother played basketball, but he never picked up on the sport. Everyone worked hard and the audience was pleased. I was overwhelmed, but just kept moving forward because there wasn't time to do anything else. Some of the actors had never danced before. There were various levels of talent, but they all worked hard to better their performances. I just kept pushing them until it was time to perform for an audience."

The cast for Stagedoor's production of *High School Musical* ranged from 15 to 16 years old, and were chosen from among those who had signed up for the summer 2006 session. In nearly every instance, the cast had no idea that Stagedoor would be taking on *HSM*, but when they were chosen, they knew they had a tremendous responsibility reinterpreting characters that had become so popular thanks to the film.

Jordan Campbell, who played Troy Bolton, explains, "I did third session at

Stagedoor and had no idea what we were going to do, but somehow my first year there I ended up in the lead role in a world premiere. I was pretty happy.

"Troy was very different from me," he says, echoing the words of the character's first alter ego, Zac Efron. "He played basketball. He liked to be in the limelight, and I do too, but he had an arrogance about him and I'm not that kind of person. I'm just an average guy. The biggest difference between us was that he's a basketball player and I'm a theater person."

He feels a primary difference between the two versions of *HSM* is that in the film if Zac messed up a line or something, they could always say "cut" and reshoot it. In the stage version, they have to be ready to do the whole thing non-stop. It's his belief that it's more of a challenge to do the whole show in one "take."

On a personal level, Jordan feels that having this particular credit on his resume will be extremely helpful, as will the fact that he attended Stagedoor Manor. "With all the press we've gotten for this show," he says, "it's been a really big deal. My ultimate goal is to be on Broadway, but I love the whole aspect of acting, whether it's television, film, singing — just everything."

Jordan's leading lady in *HSM* was Andrea Ross, who plays the part of Gabriella Montez. "The play was actually harder than I thought it would be," she admits, "because the songs are different, the script is different. I think they purposely wanted to do that to make it a little different from the film, which

I think makes it more interesting instead of seeing the whole thing over again, but just on the stage."

She also believes that her interpretation of Gabriella is different from Vanessa's, and that everyone who plays the role on stage in the future will have their own take on the character. "I definitely used Vanessa for a lot of the inspiration for some of the stuff that I did," Andrea says. "I had the movie at camp with me so if there was something I didn't understand, I could go to the movie and you could see what they did. It was a high school experience and I had done a freshman year, so it was really easy for me to relate to Gabriella being a new kid and trying to find where you belong."

In approaching the role of Sharpay, Olivia Baackes notes that the character is more comedic on stage than she was in the film. "It's all very over-the-top on stage," she

says. "Lots of energy. I loved playing Sharpay and I want to play her again, because she's just a funny character and there are always people in life who are like Sharpay. Especially in theater — every audition I go to, I see a Sharpay kind of girl, people who take themselves so seriously and are so dramatic. You just have to laugh at people like that. She was just so fun to play, because her lines are so ridiculous and funny. I definitely wanted to make Sharpay bigger, louder, funnier — like Sharpay in the movie, times ten."

Particularly thrilling for her is the impact her star role in *High School Musical* is having on her career. "On the last two auditions I've gone on, the casting directors looked at my resumé and said, 'Oh my God, you were Sharpay at Stagedoor.' People in theater are saying, 'What an opportunity,' which is true. I also got to perform for a lot of the big people at Disney, which was amazing."

A real thrill for Dylan Tedaldi, who played Sharpay's brother Ryan, is the difference between the character in the two incarnations of *HSM*. "In the movie," he begins, "you don't really see Ryan that much. Even though he's one of the main characters, he's not one who is really as obvious when you're watching him. I like the character a lot, but I wasn't thinking about him specifically when I was watching the movie. But when I got cast in the part, I really liked it a lot. Usually in shows that I'm in, I get cast as a really boring, average person, and I thought that Ryan was a really fun character for me to play, because he was really different from anything I'd done before. He was kind of evil, but he had a happy side to him. He was a little more flamboyant than other characters I've played. I think both Sharpay and Ryan were a lot different in the musical version when compared to the movie. They

game when Troy started drifting away toward Gabriella. I thought that was a pretty cool trait about him.

"It was really cool the way they adapted the music from the initial movie into more of a Broadway style," Eric continues. "I listened to the recordings of the original and the way they adapted it was sort of a revolutionary thing, because it was so poppy and mediated to be Broadway and appealing to people drawn to Broadway and the performing arts."

> "I kept about 30 percent of the dialogue and reinvented a large part of it, opening it up on stage and exploring other characters, like Sharpay and Ryan, Zeke and Kelsi."

were a lot more evil in the beginning and then they changed a bit."

Coming from a background that includes being a football and lacrosse player, a musician and a music composer, Eric Reinemann assumed the role of Chad Danforth. "I thought Chad was a high-wired guy," he opines, "really excited, always wanted to keep Troy's head in the game. He became one of the leaders of the basketball

Sarah Konowitz, who ended up playing Taylor McKessie, admits that when she attended Stagedoor for the first time in the summer of 2006, she had no idea that she would be starring in *High School Musical*.

"So when I was cast as Taylor," she enthuses, "I was so unbelievably ecstatic. I remember running over to my roommate and friend, Andrea Ross, and screaming and hugging for almost ten minutes. We were so thrilled that we were cast as best friends in the show, because of our real friendship outside of the show. Just being cast in *High School Musical* absolutely made my summer incredible."

Sarah notes that she was most definitely a fan of the film beforehand. "*HSM* combines music and dance with the values that should be most important in our lives: friendship, equality and honesty. The writers of *HSM* should be proud of their accomplishment, because nowadays it's hard to send positive messages to kids while still keeping them entertained. I think *HSM* is the perfect movie for kids to enjoy and learn from."

She admires Monique Coleman's portrayal of the character and the way that she managed to accomplish an upbeat yet sassy tone to the character. "Without copying her," explains Sarah, "I tried to use elements of Ms. Coleman's style, keeping that same optimistic energy and bold attitude. My favorite line of Taylor's is the one where she mocks the cheerleaders, because that's her more daring, forward side. She is able to stand up to the cheerleaders, without being as mean-spirited as Sharpay. In my portrayal of Taylor, I really tried to emphasize her intelligence, because it sends a good message to the audience — that success comes with hard work. Since Taylor constantly focuses on her studies and pushes Gabriella to participate in the Science Decathlon, she shows the audience that learning really matters. Because I'm a strong believer in the importance of education, I loved being able to express my feelings through playing the role of Taylor."

"My favorite line of Taylor's is the one where she mocks the cheerleaders, because that's her more daring, forward side. She is able to stand up to the cheerleaders, without being as mean-spirited as Sharpay."

In her opinion, the primary difference between the stage and film versions of *HSM* is that "the show offers more music and elaborates a little more on the points that the movie makes. For example, the song 'We're Counting On You' was added to the show version of *HSM*. I feel that this song accurately and wisely stresses the meaning of responsibility and living up to expectations. Although the movie does perfectly fine without this song, I think the play benefits from the inclusion of it."

In the end, everyone involved in the Stagedoor production of *High School Musical* is justifiably proud of their accomplishment, particularly considering that they have laid the groundwork for all the live versions to follow.

"Stagedoor has a reputation for meeting every challenge and doing the impossible," emphasizes Kittrell. "We were aware every minute of the three weeks that we had been given a unique opportunity and we rose to the occasion. The show works, it's a terrific product for communities and the messages are valid. We are very grateful to Disney and Music Theater International for giving us the chance."

Louiselle adds, "Seeing productions of the show has been gratifying. We did an Equity workshop in June and went to see Stagedoor Manor's production in August. What a hoot that was. These kids put on a fully realized production — staged, costumed, choreographed — in twelve days!"

"I hope the kids who know every line of the movie will have fun discovering the new changes and additions to the story," Simpatico muses, "and will allow themselves to engage with the live version. And of course I hope they have a blast performing the piece and finding their own expression, rather than copying the fine performances in the movie. It's all about expression."

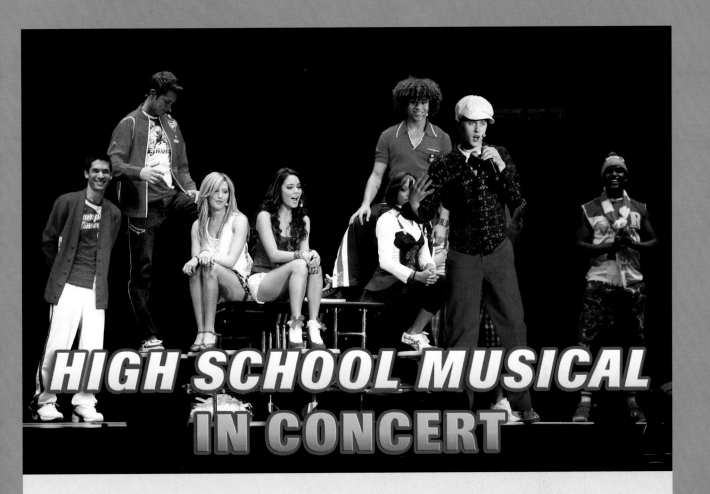

HIGH SCHOOL MUSICAL IN CONCERT

How many times can a franchise be successfully reinvented? Well, Disney is rapidly discovering that there may not be a limit for *High School Musical*. The TV movie — so popular its soundtrack sold four million copies and its DVD over two million copies — has stage shows springing up at high schools around the country, Broadway and theme park versions in the works, and for fans lucky enough to get tickets, *High School Musical: The Concert*.

To keep things fresh, this production, supervised by *HSM* director Kenny Ortega, is not just a recreation of the film and its storyline on stage. Instead, it's a concert — pure and simple. Original cast members Vanessa Anne Hudgens, Ashley Tisdale, Corbin Bleu, Monique Coleman and Lucas Grabeel all participated in the tour. The only no-show was Zac Efron, who was off filming the musical *Hairspray*; in his place was Drew Seeley, who co-wrote some of the film's songs and whose voice was blended in with Zac's. All of the numbers from *HSM* were performed during the 90-minute show, as were original tunes from the solo albums of Vanessa, Ashley and Corbin. The sold-out 40-city tour began on November 30, 2006, in San Diego, California, and concluded on January 28, 2007, in Las Vegas, Nevada.

The cast of *High School Musical* run through a dress rehearsal on November 28, 2006, for the live tour, which began the next day in San Diego. Drew Seeley (bottom left) played the part of Troy.

Probably the nicest surprise of all was critics' response to the show; they seemed to be enjoying it as much as the audience. Offered *The San Francisco Chronicle,* "*High School Musical* is meant for singing along, and the audience was always reminded of familiar themes, with scenes from the movie playing out on the IMAX-sized video screen at the back of the stage. . . . The production served as a coming-out for the actors and actresses, providing an opportunity to distance themselves from their *High School* counterparts. Lucas Grabeel, whose Ryan Evans character is sort of sniveling, turns out to be a solid Seacrest-style emcee in real life, holding the event together with his upbeat banter. Hudgens is the Kelly Clarkson of the bunch, and we mean that in a good way."

Added the *San Jose Mercury News*, "The high-energy, sugary-sweet performance was visually and musically dazzling, full of upbeat hip-hop dance moves, showy special effects and the exuberant show tunes–style music that made the movie's soundtrack the best-selling CD of the year . . . Disney spared no expense on special effects, sets or costumes. The gigantic screen behind the stage alternated between showing clips of the movie, live video of singers on stage and video of audience members — all of which successfully integrated the concert, the film and the viewers."

The sensational concert tour suggests that *High School Musical* fans will be welcoming reinventions of the franchise for some time to come.

THE GANG'S ALL HERE
High School Musical 2

At the beginning of 2007, Vanessa Anne Hudgens, Zac Efron, Ashley Tisdale, Corbin Bleu, Monique Coleman and Lucas Grabeel moved away from their individual careers so that they could come back in front of the *High School Musical* cameras as the sequel began shooting under the direction of the returning Kenny Ortega.

"It's supposed to take place during summer vacation, and we're supposed to be at a country club, so it should be pretty interesting," Corbin Bleu said at the Teen Choice Awards.

"All I can tell you," says Disney Channel's Michael Healy, "is it probably won't be based at the school. It will be a whole new journey, but it will be the same friends along for the ride. The line we're using around work is, 'School's out, but the show must go on.'"

Elaborates writer Peter Barsocchini, "For one thing, we didn't want to try to imitate *High School Musical*. We wanted to do something fresh. It begins on the last day of

"It will be a whole new journey, but it will be the same friends along for the ride. The line we're using around work is, 'School's out, but the show must go on.'"

school and it does take place over the summer and the characters find themselves in some new situations. When I was thinking about a sequel, I said, 'What do you think would happen if Sharpay suddenly took a strong interest in Troy?'"

HSM 2 reportedly finds Troy (Zac), Gabriella (Vanessa), Sharpay (Ashley), Ryan (Lucas), Chad (Corbin) and Taylor (Monique) organizing a talent show at the local country and golf club to which Sharpay and Ryan's family belongs, and where Troy is working the summer as a lifeguard.

Jealous of the attention that Troy's and Gabriella's newfound talents have received, Ryan and Sharpay set out to restore the "natural balance" of life. They plot to break up Troy and Gabriella so they won't be in the

"To tell you the truth, the whole thing was kind of an accident. I don't know what you've heard, but Troy and Gabriella *did* kiss at the end of the movie."

spotlight. In order to do that, Sharpay fakes drowning at the pool, which means lifeguard Troy has to give Sharpay mouth-to-mouth. At the same time, Ryan convinces Gabriella that Troy is cheating on her with Sharpay.

"The tease is, 'School's out for summer,'" Zac says about the sequel, which producers say will test the characters' true feelings and trust for one another.

Zac himself teases fans by addressing the question of why Troy and Gabriella didn't kiss at the end of the first film. He laughs, "When I first saw the movie, I didn't even notice there wasn't a kiss! I guess it's implied. To tell you the truth, the whole thing was kind of an accident. I don't know what you've heard, but Troy and Gabriella *did* kiss at the end of the movie. However, leaving it out of the final movie left some intrigue. Now you'll just have to watch the sequel to find out what happens!"

Although it's just conjecture on their part, the film's cast members have shared their thoughts on the sequel. Zac says, "I would like to do more dancing in the new one. I loved when people were doing flips and cartwheels on cafeteria tables — it looked like so much fun. I wish I was more involved with those numbers. With Troy, I think there's not much more I can ask for. If Troy gets any cooler, he'll explode. I wish I was more like him. He can just keep on doing what he's doing. And all the stuff that we've been doing as far as promoting and going to New York and traveling the world is fun, but I think filming the movie was really where the magic happened. It's all represented when we were filming that last number ['We're All in This Together']. So I can't wait to go back and experience that one more time with all my friends."

Vanessa shares, "I think I'd like to see Gabriella come out of her shell a little more, because she's very shy and she likes to hide behind her books. Now that she's accomplished something in front of her school, I think I want her to maybe be a little more spontaneous."

"They are talking about me singing a solo song," Corbin explains. "I definitely think we're going to have solo songs, especially because I'm going to be coming out with an album, so that is definitely something that I am going to be working on. They definitely said they were open to it and I know that it's something I've wanted to do. I would also love Chad to try a new activity so he does not exactly revolve only around basketball. That would be really cool and it would let us see a whole new side of him."

Lucas admits, "I'm looking forward to coming together again in a different light. This time we're not going to have those two weeks where we have to get to know each

> "It's going to be 'wham, bam, thank you ma'am' for the sequel as far as connecting and working with each other again."

other or anything. And especially being in such close proximity to the actual shooting of the movie and now all this publicity and press that we've done, we've really gotten to know each other. It's going to be 'wham, bam, thank you ma'am' for the sequel as far as connecting and working with each other again."

There are millions of *High School Musical* fans out there who are literally counting the days until the sequel's premiere and doing whatever they can to stay connected to their new heroes. Needless to say, the phenomenon continues.

Regarding that phenomenon, director Kenny Ortega notes, "Timing is everything. I've always said that *High School Musical* owes a lot to the cast, which was really focused and able to accomplish more than

we should have been allowed to do in the time we were given. It was an incredible cast, brilliant marketing and kids found the story accessible. You can go for years and not find this kind of synergy."

"Every decade has had an iconic musical: *West Side Story, Grease, Phantom of the Opera, Rent*," adds Disney's Gary Marsh. "I'm hoping *High School Musical* becomes iconic for this decade. I believe 20 years from now kids will talk about this musical the way we talk about *Grease*. The film speaks to peer pressure, the cost of following your dreams. We were able to take those themes and embed them in world-class songs. Music is a huge part of kids' lives. There's no reason to believe this film was a fluke."